Abdullah Hakeem: Cherishing a Sweet Legacy 7-14 years

by Umm Assad

This book belongs to

_____

Copyright © 2024CE/1445H Umm Assad Publications
All rights reserved. No part of this publication may be reproduced, stored in a retrieval system, or transmitted in any form or by any means, electronic, mechanical, photocopying, recording or otherwise, without the prior permission of the copyright owner.

This book is not intended as a replacement for seeking knowledge. The reader is advised to take full responsibility for safeguarding their knowledge and understanding of Tawheed by regularly referring to authentic sources such as the Quran, Sahih Ahadith, studying books of Scholars and their trusted students and other than that in the matters relating to his/her religion (Islam).

A catalogue record for this book is available from the British Library.

ISBN-13:	978-1-915233-20-2
ISBN-10:	1915233208
Author	Umm Assad Bint Jamil Mohammed
Checked by	Abu Isma'eel Mustafa George DeBerry
Published on	2024CE/1445H

ummassadpublications.com

Contents

Chapter 1: A Tree of Solace
Chapter 2: The Sad News
Chapter 3: Heart-to-Heart
Chapter 4: The Janazah
Chapter 5: Hearts United
Chapter 6: Staying Up Late
Chapter 7: The Supplications
Chapter 8: Changes and More Changes
Chapter 9: A Promise to Keep
Chapter 10: Time to Bid Farewell
Chapter 11: Learning from Grandpa Luqman
Chapter 12: Grandpa Luqman's Acceptance
Chapter 13: A Legacy of Love
Chapter 14: Sweet Memories
Chapter 15: Whispers in The Dark
Chapter 16: Unexpected Turns
Chapter 17: Shopping with Ummi
Chapter 18: The Queen's Fate
Chapter 19: New Supplies, New Hope
Chapter 20: Abdullah's Big Day
Bonus Chapter: The Gift of Wisdom

Bismillahir-Rahmanir-Raheem. Indeed, all praise is for Allah. We praise Him; we seek His Help, and we seek His Forgiveness. We seek refuge with Allah from the evil of our own souls and the consequence of our actions. Whomsoever Allah guides, nobody can misguide and whomsoever Allah misguides nobody can guide. I testify that none has the right to be worshipped except Allah alone, He has no partners, and I testify that Muhammad is His slave and Messenger.

Dear Parents, Teachers and Guardians,

Asalaamu Alaykom and welcome to a journey rooted in real-life stories and true events. In the pages of this book, you'll find stories that have inspired, shaped, and touched the lives of many. To respect privacy, I have altered names and details, yet I've strived to preserve the authenticity of the historical and emotional experiences shared.

Please be aware that the story delves into themes of loss and grief, which, while important, may be sensitive for younger readers. This book aims not only to entertain but also to foster understanding and empathy. I hope it serves as a valuable starting point for conversations with your children about these profound life experiences.

Thank you for sharing this journey with us.

May Allaah bless you all,

Umm Assad

DEDICATION

To all those that stand united upon Tawheed and implementation of the Sunnah of the Prophet Muhammadﷺ, may Allaah grant us all the strength of Iman and health, physical, mental and emotional strength, patience and gratitude so we can worship Him alone and correctly! *Ameen.*

Umm Assad.

Welcome to the world of the Hakeem Family,

Meet Grandpa Luqman:

Raised on a farm, he met his sweet wife many years ago through their shared love for the Quran and Sunnah, (and honey), shaping his profound insights. Abdullah's wise and beloved grandfather, favourite mentor and friend, brings a lifetime of wisdom and an unbreakable bond.

Meet Abbi:

The family's guiding light, expertly balances farm life, faith, and community. Respected for his empathy, he's a true leader at home and in the community. Additionally, Abbi turns to gardening as a way to channel his anger, finding peace in nature.

Meet Abdullah:

An introverted, curious young boy who loves learning about Islam and the world around him. He cherishes family time and tending to his bees. His quiet nature and distinctive look make it difficult to connect with others, yet he never gives up easily.

Meet Yusuf:

Yusuf, Abdullah's best friend, is a smart and confident boy with a love for adventure. His steadfast loyalty and fearless attitude make him an invaluable companion.

where love, wisdom, and adventure await!

Meet Grandma Jamila:
A woman of warmth and wisdom, she shared her love through her expert knowledge of honey and her nurturing spirit. Her legacy of kindness and devotion continues to inspire Abdullah and his family.

Meet Ummi:
The heart of the home; a devoted mother who ensures everything runs smoothly. Although sometimes goes unnoticed, her daily routine and care for her family make her home a sanctuary of warmth.

Meet Ramlah:
A sweet 5-year-old, is the family's bundle of joy. She adores her big brother Abdullah and brings innocence and energy to every moment.

Meet Miza:
The family's sleek and active cat, offers silent companionship with her emerald-green eyes, often surprising everyone with her loud meows.

Meet the Honeybees:
And don't forget these amazing creatures, small yet mighty, vital for our ecosystem.

"Great things happen when the energy of the youth work together with the wisdom of the elders."
– Grandpa Luqman

Chapter 1:
A Tree of Solace

As the evening prayer (Maghrib) neared, the setting sun painted the peaceful countryside with a warm, golden glow on the horizon.

Abdullah Hakeem, an eleven-year-old home-schooled boy, lived on the farm with his parents, little sister Ramlah, goats, chickens, and a playful cat called Miza.

One day, he stood tall beneath his favourite tree, feeling the branches gently brush against his small afro that crowned his head due to his height. His tanned skin bore witness to countless hours spent near his tree of comfort. He was a blend of Arab and Ethiopian heritage, which he cherished. And his unique charm included a rare feature – vitiligo, which appeared as faint patches of skin on his hands and face.

Abdullah's vitiligo was discovered at a young age. His family, especially his grandparents, have always provided a supportive environment. At first, he was self-conscious about these unique markings, but as he grew older, his wise Grandpa Luqman used to tell him stories of how uniqueness is celebrated in their culture and how these patches make him more special.

As Abdullah stretched out his hand to reach a branch with a nest of honeybees, he observed the depigmented patches on his skin and compared himself to them. He felt a connection to them, a bond nurtured by his Grandma Jamila during the spring season. It was as if he could understand their world.

A gentle breeze passed by, causing the fabric of his three-quarter length trousers to sway, proudly reflecting his adherence to the Prophet's (peace and blessings be upon him) teachings on lower garment length for men and boys, an important part of his Muslim identity.

Approaching the beehive eagerly, as he did every day, Abdullah observed the bees' hard work with wide eyes behind his rounded glasses. Fascinated, he watched as they carefully went about their work, gathering nectar from flowers and buzzing around. Their busy activities captivated him, drawing him close to the hives in awe.

As an introvert, he cherished quiet moments, finding solace in nature, books, and reflection, rather than in noisy games. One of his most cherished hobbies was camping. Every year, upon completing his final Islamic lesson, his father Abbi promises a camping trip as a reward for his hard work. This year, camping included not just his family but his best friend, Yusuf, a home-schooled student from his Islamic class.

This summer, Abdullah had been working hard on an important presentation for his homework. It required each student to select an animal mentioned in the Quran, studying it, memorising the relevant verse, and presenting their findings in class. Inspired by his grandmother's fascination with bees, he chose them as his topic. She had promised to guide him in his exploration, which he was incredibly excited about.

Continuing to observe his buzzy bees, Abdullah noticed a struggling bee and he went to fetch a small leaf. He gently placed the tired insect on the hive, a small act of kindness that deepened his bond with these incredible creatures and planted the seeds of his love for them. When he returned to the beehive, it looked different.

Confused, he noticed several honeycombs missing, and wondered if it was a natural occurrence or if someone had taken them.

As Abdullah settled back under his tree, he gazed at the horizon in reflection, by his small, golden farm with fields stretched out, overlooking the distant city. On the far edge of his home, past the swaying crops, lay the home of his rather unfriendly neighbour, Patrick Lucas.

Patrick's dislike for children, especially when they played near his wildflower meadow, was well-known in the neighbourhood. His impatience and hearing loss in one ear made him challenging to communicate with. Yet, there was a ray of kindness behind his harshness – Fiona Lucas, Patrick's wife. Fiona struggles with a persistent cough. Despite their issues, they were known to be exceptionally quiet neighbours when left alone.

"Abdullah! Time for Maghrib!" Abbi, called. He couldn't help but sense his father's tone was a little different. Abbi had been acting strange lately, though Abdullah couldn't quite understand why.

Abbi, a strong man with a strong build from tending their small farm had been spending more time at home gardening, which was his way of releasing pent-up anger. He found solace in the farm.

"Yes, Abbi! I'm coming!" Abdullah replied, turning around annoyed to see his cheeky little sister, Ramlah, sneaking up on him, causing him to jump. "Subhan Allah," he exclaimed. He didn't expect to see her there.

Ramlah tugged on her brother's sleeve, looking up to him with her innocent eyes. Her doll, Laila, had lost her tiny shoe, and they needed to find it before Maghrib.

Reluctant to sacrifice his quiet time at first, Abdullah decided not to let down his little sister, and promised, "Let's look together, Ramlah, until we find Laila's shoe."

Ramlah smiled at her big brother, knowing that if anyone could solve this little mystery, it was him. They shared a special bond - Ramlah's cheerful laughter that spread joy, and Abdullah's patience that inspired her every day. And so, they set off on an adventure around the farm, looking through every corner and gap.

After some searching, they discovered Laila's tiny shoe hidden in the tall grass, just in time for Maghrib. Nearby, they noticed a pile of soil that appeared slightly raised and disturbed, but Abdullah paid no attention to it, recalling his father's recent gardening.

Ramlah took the opportunity to explore the fascinating world of her doll's tiny shoe, her imagination at play. Abdullah, however, felt growing impatience as Abbi's persistent calls pushed him to get ready for prayer time at the Masjid. Ramlah looked up with disappointment in her eyes, but with determination, Abdullah quickly comforted her with a promise of playtime tomorrow.

As Abbi's third call echoed through the house, Mr. Lucas passed by, looking visibly troubled from a bad day. He instructed Abdullah to see his father and warned him to stay away from his crops. Meanwhile, he carried a pot of freshly made soup for his sick wife, a special recipe by his grandma, cooked by Abdullah's mother, Ummi, both of whom are Palestinian.

Abdullah, aware of Mr. Lucas' rudeness, still responded kindly, recalling his mother's teachings about kindness to neighbours, "Yes, Mr. Lucas. I hope Mrs. Lucas enjoys the soup. Made especially for her," he said.

He quickly turned back towards Ramlah, grinned, and silently asked Allah (The Most High) to guide Mr. Lucas. With Laila's found shoe, Abdullah took Ramlah's hand and ran through the soil paths to the house together.

With the beauty of the sun setting, Abdullah could smell his mother's delicious cooking in the breeze and couldn't help but reflect on how blessed he was.

Their peaceful rural home was a blend of family-time, hard work, and appreciating the world around them. Despite having different personalities and hobbies, the Hakeem family all shared a love for learning the Quran and Sunnah, which made Abdullah's life truly special.

Through the window, Abdullah's sharp eyes caught a glimpse of his father on the phone, pacing back and forth with an unsettled look on his face. Abdullah couldn't help but wonder what was going on. Sensing something was wrong, he entered his home and approached his father. "Abbi, is grandpa coming with us to the Masjid today?" he asked, concern in his voice.

His father paused, with the phone conversation still fresh in his mind. "Not today, son. Grandpa is, you know, a bit tired, but we'll catch up with him soon, insha'Allah," Abbi replied, trying to mask his worry with a reassuring smile. "We're taking the open-bed truck today 'cause we're running late." Abbi continued.

Abdullah, sensing an unusual tension yet respecting his father's words, nodded as he set off to perform Wudhu. The unanswered questions lingered in his mind.

Little did he know that this peaceful world was about to undergo a profound change—one that would test his resilience and faith in ways he could never imagine.

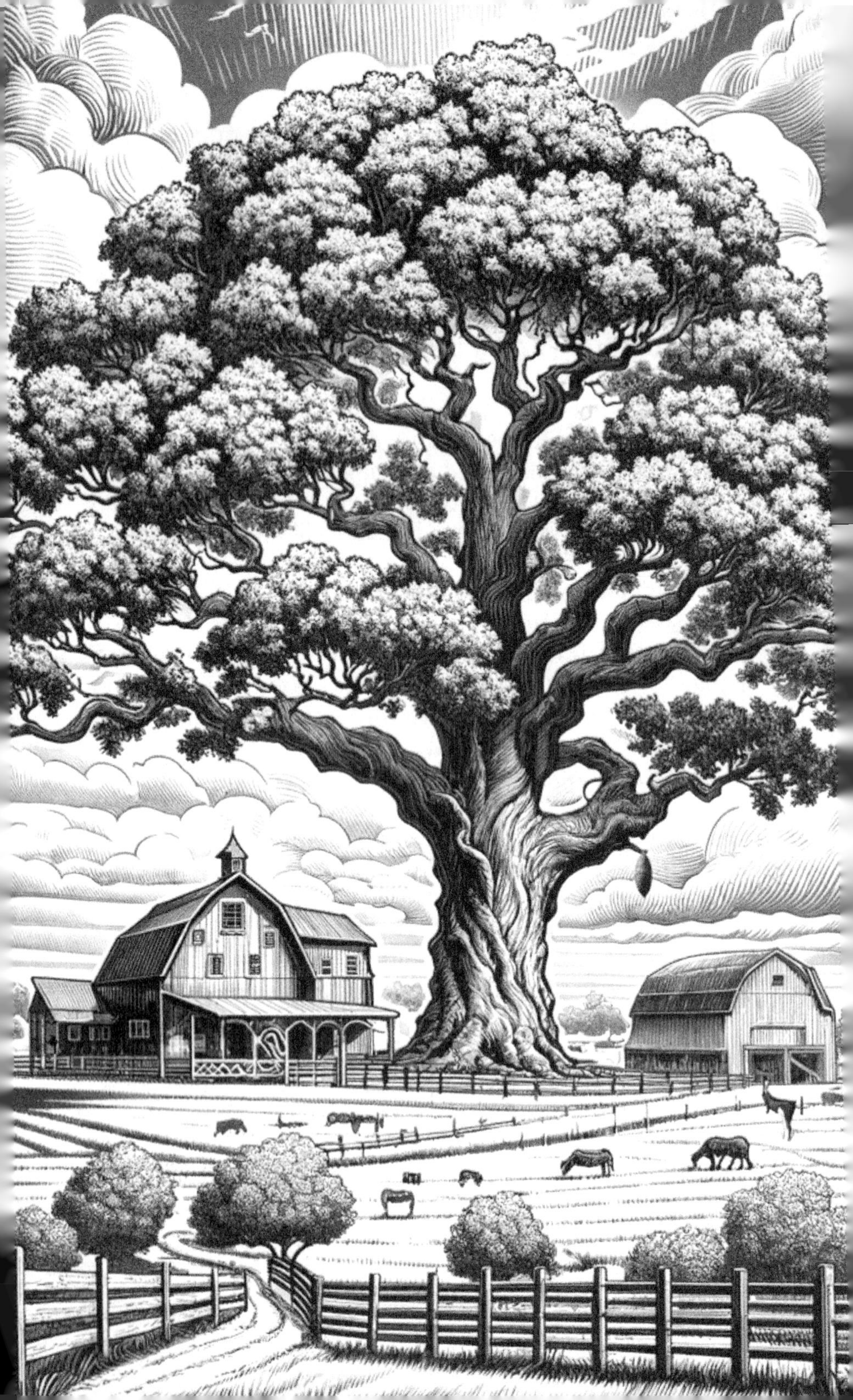

Chapter 2:
The Sad News

Abdullah and Abbi prepared for the Maghrib prayer at the local Masjid. Abbi applied his usual touch of perfume behind his ears, then lightly splashed some on Abdullah's sleeve as a final touch. He smiled at Abdullah, trying to maintain a positive and strong attitude. "We'll be back by dinner, Aish, insha'Allah," he assured Abdullah's mother.

"You want some rice?" Ummi asked, confused.
"No, I meant 'Aish,'" Abbi clarified gently.
"Oh, sorry, I'm just tired. That reminds me, I forgot to cook the rice." Ummi stated, seeing them off.

As they set off for their prayer at the Masjid, Abdullah noticed his parents behaving differently. Abbi was typically cheerful, and Ummi was usually good at remembering things but today they seemed slightly out of character. Abdullah couldn't quite pinpoint it, but he decided to wait and see if anything was bothering them.

"Yallah, Habibi," Abbi gently encouraged Abdullah, his mind deep in thought as they head towards the Masjid door. The congregation sparked a sense of unity and peace as they prayed together. Abdullah felt connected to his faith and the community, which was comforting given his unease about his father's behaviour.

After the prayer, as they made their way back home, Abbi halted outside the house and took a deep breath. Abdullah watched his father closely, sensing that something important was about to happen.

Eager to break the silence, Abdullah playfully prodded Abbi, "How about a quick race? Last one out of the truck is a... well, you know, king of the barn!"

This game had been their favourite to play together since Abdullah was just a toddler. It meant cleaning up animal waste in the barns, a tough and messy job. But sadly today, Abbi refused to join in.

As Abdullah was ready to step out of the truck with his hand on the door handle, he suddenly noticed the gravity in Abbi's expression, and the truck fell into an awkward silence. He let go of the door handle and remained seated, nervously scratching his head in embarrassment and confusion.

"Abdullah, Habibi," Abbi began slowly, his voice mixed with sadness, "I want to talk to you about something." He paused, carefully selecting his words.

Abdullah, still trying to grasp his father's unusual behaviour, nodded politely.

Abbi continued, "You know how we learn life's lessons from the Quran and the Sunnah, right?"

Abdullah nodded again, curious about where his father was leading the conversation.

Abbi leaned in, his eyes holding a gentle curiosity, and asked, "Abdullah, what do you know about Tawheed?"

Abdullah, reflecting the gravity of his thoughts, replied, "Tawheed means Oneness. There are three categories of Tawheed (Oneness); Oneness of the Lordship of Allah, Oneness in the worship of Allah, and Oneness in Allah's Names and Attributes."

Abbi smiled, appreciating his son's grasp of the religion. "And tell me about the Oneness of Allah's Lordship."

Abdullah, eager to share his knowledge, began, "There are five categories in the Oneness of the Lordship of Allah; Allah alone Creates, Allah alone Provides, Allah Sustains all His creation, Allah alone is the Owner of us all, and someday we will all return to Him."

Abbi paused for a moment, thinking about Abdullah's words. Then he gently interrupted, "Stop right there. That's what I want to talk with you about, Habibi. That Allah (The Most High) is the Creator and Owner of us all, so someday we will return to Him."

Abdullah's eyes widened with concern. He looked at his father, fully focused on his next words, ready to take in the news he was about to receive.

Abbi then asked, "Similarly, if you borrowed something from a friend, he has the right to take it back, right?"

Abdullah pondered for a moment. "Right," he replied.

Abbi gave a soft nod. "Similarly, we shared many special memories with Grandma Jamila. Yet tonight, she returned to Allah (The Most High)."

Abdullah's biggest inspirations in life were his Grandma Jamila and Grandpa Luqman. From them, he learned invaluable life skills, discovering wisdom, love, and empathy in their teachings that shaped his character, personality and even his lifegoals.

Abdullah's eyes widened further as the weight of his father's words settled in. "Grandma Jamila... passed away?" he asked, his voice trembling.

Abbi replied, comforting Abdullah. "Yes, Habibi," he said softly. "It was her time to go. We must remember her in our prayers and cherish the time we had with her. *Prophet Muhammad (peace and blessings be upon him) shed tears at the death of his young son and he said, 'Crying is a mercy! The eyes shed tears, the heart feels sad, but we do not speak except for that which pleases our Lord.'*"

Abdullah felt a mix of emotions – sadness, confusion, and a deep sense of loss. While the topic of death was a common reminder within their home, he had never experienced the death of a loved one before, and it was a profound moment for him. But as his father's words of faith resonated with him, Abdullah found a glimmer of understanding in the midst of his grief.

"To Allah we belong and to Him we shall all return," Abdullah recited.

Together, father and son sat under the fading sunlight, sharing a moment of reflection and remembrance of Grandma Jamila. It marked the beginning of Abdullah's journey to grasp the concept of death and the importance of cherishing time spent with loved ones.

Abbi, seeing the sadness merge from Abdullah's eyes, moved in to hug him. Abdullah sat, frozen. Abbi immediately sensed Abdullah's reluctance in that moment. Respecting his space, Abbi rested his hand upon Abdullah's shoulder, offering silent support.

Abdullah had always been one to value his personal space, allowing him to process things in his own time and at his own pace. It wasn't that he disliked his own father; rather, he needed a moment alone to process his emotions privately, and Abbi knew this about him.

"May Allah magnify our reward, and make perfect our bereavement, and forgive her. We must be patient and anticipate His reward! Alhamdulillah, Grandma Jamila died upon Tawheed and Sunnah!" Abbi wiped away a teardrop as he reassured Abdullah.

Abdullah asked if his mother knew, and Abbi nodded, mentioning how they would all get through this experience together.

As the summer evening turned into night, the Hakeem family gathered at home for dinner, their faces revealing the news of Grandma Jamila's passing.

With wide, innocent eyes, Ramlah asked, "Abdullah, why do you look so sad? Want to play with my toy?"

Barely finishing half his plate, Abdullah stood up and excused himself, mentioning that he was going to bed early, despite his mother having cooked his favourite Palestinian dish, Maqluba, and Kanafeh for dessert.

Ummi, concerned, watched Abdullah walk away. "Abdullah?" she called softly, wanting to comfort him.

"Aisha..." Abbi quietly pleaded Ummi, suggesting that they allow Abdullah some personal space.

"Is Abdullah mad at me?" Ramlah asked, worried.

"No, sweetie," Ummi replied, gently kissing her cheek. "Abdullah is just thinking. He's not mad at you."

As Abdullah left the room, his loyal cat Miza sensed his sadness and quietly trailed him up the stairs. Just as he climbed, a creaky step gave way, causing him to stumble and adding to his sorrow.

Abbi couldn't help but startle when he witnessed Abdullah's stumble on the creaky stair. He exchanged a guilty look with Ummi. Their inability to fix the broken steps was a constant source of frustration, especially since they had recently been burdened by Abbi's job loss due to company downsizing. Ummi, a dedicated stay-at-home mother and home-schooler to her children, had never worked outside their modest home.

Overwhelmed with embarrassment, Abbi promised to use his small savings to repair the stairs. Prioritising his family's safety and comfort, he committed to fixing the stairs despite their financial struggles.

"I promise to fix those stairs no matter what, insha'Allah." Abbi said decisively.

With a heavy heart, Ummi said to Abbi, "Perhaps we should've waited until after dinner to tell him," her voice tinged with feelings of guilt and regret.

"It's okay, Aish, we couldn't have known. We'll speak to him after he's had time to think, insha'Allah." Abbi embraced Ummi, understanding the unspoken sorrow.

Abdullah entered his room, and by his bedside, he performed the evening prayer (Isha). Right after, he performed the night prayer (Witr), his Dua (supplication) to Allah (The Most High) filled with longing for mercy, before sinking into his bed. The memory of his beloved grandmother, now gone, weighed heavily on his young heart. The void her passing had left seemed to cast a shadow over him.

Miza followed him, curling up at his feet, mirroring his sadness. As he lay there, deep in reflection, the night quietly slipped away.

Chapter 3: Heart-to-Heart

The rays of dawn gently filtered through Abdullah's bedroom window. It was the first morning after the news of Grandma Jamila's passing, with her Janazah (funeral) scheduled for later that day. As he woke up from his sleep, he was moved by the familiar sound of his roosters crowing "COCK-A-DOODLE-DOO."

Shortly after, he heard the gentle calling of his mother's voice. "Abdullah, it's time for your morning routine!"

Abdullah was accustomed to this routine; it had been instilled in him since childhood. He sat up, feeling the cool morning air, and began with the morning Dua, praising Allah (The Most High) and seeking His blessings and guidance for the day ahead.

Following that, a brisk cold shower refreshed his senses, preparing him for the day. As he dressed for the day, Abdullah reached for his special sunscreen on the dresser. With gentle care, he applied a protective layer over the delicate patches of his vitiligo-prone skin. It was a daily habit, *"a shield against the sun's harsh rays,"* as his mother always says, ensuring his skin remained healthy and vibrant. Then, with devotion, he recited his portion of the Quran, his voice melodious in the silence of the morning.

Meanwhile, his parents, who had been awake for a while, tended to the farm's daily chores, feeding the animals, milking the goats, and collecting fresh eggs from the hens.

After praying Fajr at the local Masjid, breakfast followed. It featured a hearty Palestinian meal called Shakshouka, traditionally eaten with their fingers. The meal included bread, dips, cheeses, boiled eggs, olives, and a freshly made salad of sliced tomatoes and cucumbers – a nourishing feast for the body.

Abdullah understood that this routine was more than mere tasks; it was a means of disciplining oneself, mentally, academically, physically, as well as spiritually. Ummi had always emphasised its importance to her children. Even on this quiet, gloomy morning, she did her best to keep up their familiar routine.

And so, as Abdullah headed down the stairs, he knew that this well-practiced routine was the foundation upon which his day would begin.

Sitting in the dimly lit living room, he awaited the trip to the local Masjid for Fajr prayer with his father and grandfather. His gaze drifted to the hallway, landing on a framed photograph from last year's camping trip.

As Abbi prepared for their journey, Abdullah remained still, lost in his thoughts, the pain of losing his beloved grandmother was noticeable. It was a heavy burden he couldn't shake, making conversation with his family an unbearable task. In the quiet moment, he found peace and silently contemplated the memories of his grandmother, yearning for her presence.

Ummi and Abbi exchanging understanding glances, quietly approached him, and offered him seven Ajwa dates as a protection against evil. Abdullah gratefully accepted, his smile fragile yet genuine. His parents' efforts to respect his grieving process didn't go unnoticed.

The doorbell rang, and Abbi rushed to answer it. As he swung the door open, there stood Grandpa Luqman, now his widowed father, and Abdullah's favourite person since childhood.

Even though their homes were separated by just one street, they were always ready to head to the Masjid together as they had for the past 5 years, grandfather, father, and grandson.

With a warm smile, Grandpa Luqman addressed his son by his first name, saying, "O Aslam, how quickly time passes, my son."

Abbi, touched by the familiarity of his father's words, fully embraced him. He insisted that they stay together through the difficult day. However, Grandpa Luqman, with a distant look in his eyes, gently declined. He yearned for some moments of solitude to reflect on the memories of his beloved departed wife after they prayed Fajr together. Abbi, understanding the need, respectfully agreed to part ways thereafter with the promise to meet later. Each carried their own thoughts and memories of the loved one they were about to pray the Janazah prayer over.

Hours later, the Hakeem family proceeded to the local Masjid for the Janazah, their hearts heavy from the loss, and the atmosphere gloomy around them. It was a difficult and nerve-racking experience for them all.

Under the hot summer sun, Abdullah sat on an old wooden bench outside the Masjid, moments before Grandma Jamila's Janazah. Staring at the ground as he tried to come to terms with the loss of his sweet grandmother, he had been keeping his distance from his family since the sad news, lost in his own thoughts.

Grandpa Luqman provided comforting presence during this difficult time. Understanding his grandson's inner battle, he slowly moved to sit beside him. He inhaled deeply, his eyes filled with wisdom and empathy.

"Abdullah," Grandpa Luqman used a calm, reassuring tone, "This is a difficult time for all of us. Losing Grandma Jamila is a heavy burden, especially on your young shoulders." Abdullah remained silent, his gaze still fixed on the ground.

Grandpa Luqman continued, "You don't have to carry this weight alone, my boy. In our family, we're here for one another. We share our joys and our sorrows, and that's what makes us strong." Abdullah's eyes welled up with tears, but he didn't speak.

Placing a comforting hand on Abdullah's shoulder, Grandpa Luqman whispered, "It's okay to feel upset. Keep in mind that *Allah does not punish for shedding tears, nor for the grief of the heart.*"

Abdullah looked up at his grandfather, his eyes filled with sadness and gratitude. He couldn't find the words, but he felt the weight of his grandfather's words sink in. Grandpa Luqman smiled at Abdullah. "You know, your grandma was so excited about helping you with your homework. Before she passed away, she asked me to give this note to you."

As Grandpa Luqman handed Abdullah the note, his eyes lit up, recognising his grandmothers familiar handwriting:
         "Surah 16, Ayah 68-70."

"Looks like the reference about bees," Abdullah noted, pausing briefly. "Hold on, there's more," he continued.

Upon closer inspection, he discovered additional words from his grandmother beneath the reference:

"A sweet legacy awaits you; patience is key."

Abdullah smiled. "Grandma promised to help with my presentation, and she kept her word," he said. "She's gone, yet I feel her legacy will live on, insha'Allah."

A single tear trickled slowly down Grandpa Luqman's weathered cheek. He reached into his pocket, seeking his cherished handkerchief, but it was not there. "Now, where is my handkerchief? I'm certain it was in my pocket this morning," Grandpa Luqman muttered.

Abdullah quickly fetched a tissue from his pocket, offering it to Grandpa Luqman with empathy. "Here, Grandpa," he said softly.

Grandpa Luqman, struggling slightly to hear, leaned closer. "May Allah (The Most High) bless you, my boy," he said, his voice tinged with gratitude. "You're always so thoughtful." He accepted the tissue, a glimmer of appreciation in his eyes.

Amidst the heartfelt moment, only Abdullah, with his keen observations, caught this subtle change in his beloved grandfather. He had never seen him weep like this before, except for the mention of the end of times. "Even the strong cry," he thought.

As they sat there, two generations apart yet connected by their love for Grandma Jamila, Abdullah began to realise the truth in his grandfather's words. He might still find it challenging to express his feelings, but he knew he had a family that would always be there to support him when he needed it most.

Moments before Grandma Jamila's Janazah, the ache weighed heavily on Abdullah's broken heart. Slowly, he moved closer to his parents, his eyes glistening with unshed tears. He felt the need to apologise for his recent distance and moments of selfishness, which seemed petty in the face of their loss. Hesitating, he whispered, "I'm sorry, Ummi, Abbi, for... you know, not being understanding."

His parents exchanged understanding looks, knowing the hardship that Abdullah had been dealing with. Ummi gently placed a hand on his cheek and said, "Abdullah, my dear, there's no need for you to apologise. We all grieve in our own ways, and you've been strong."

Abbi, with a faint smile, chimed in, "And I'm sorry for delivering the news to you before you even had a chance to finish your dinner. How thoughtless of me!" He hugged Abdullah and patted his back, trying to connect through the difficulty.

In that moment, they found solace in each other's presence, hoping that they would navigate this challenging time together as a family should.

Ramlah, with her innocence, tugged at Abdullah's sleeve, her watery eyes reflecting her confusion amidst the sadness. She whispered, "Why is everyone sad?"

Abdullah knelt down, gently wiping away her tears, and explained, "We're sad because Grandma Jamila has returned to Allah (The Most High), and we are all going to miss her." Ramlah nodded, her tiny hand clutching her brother's, while her other hand held her favourite doll, finding comfort in his reassurance during this difficult moment.

Chapter 4:
The Janazah

Family, friends and members of the community had gathered to prepare for Grandma Jamila's Janazah, following the Islamic customs. As they proceeded to the Janazah, the sun shone brightly, yet they carried a heaviness in their hearts. It was a bittersweet moment.

Abdullah, holding Ramlah's hand, felt a mixture of emotions. The faces around him were a blend of familiar and unfamiliar, all sharing in the grief of losing Grandma Jamila, as well as serving as a powerful reminder that someday it would be them buried in the ground and questioned for all they used to do.

One by one, Abdullah's relatives arrived at the Janazah. Suddenly, an older relative they hadn't seen in a while, Uncle Musa, arrived with his son, Umar, who came from the busy city life.

"Musa! It's been too long," Abbi greeted his brother.

Uncle Musa smiled back, signs of regret on his face, "Indeed, Aslam. We've been so busy. Proud to see my younger brother make a life for himself out here, just as you always said you would. Always the wise one."

"The wise one?" Abdullah mused quietly. A spark ignited within him, stirring a desire to be wise.

Abbi sighed. "Well, I'm glad you could make it. Times like these make you reflect, don't they?" Abbi and Musa exchanged glances, recognising their shared sorrow.

Uncle Musa agreed, "Yes, they do. Right, Umar?" He gave a gentle nudge to his son, who nodded quietly.

It had been years since their last meeting, so Uncle Musa was surprised to see how much Abdullah and Ramlah had grown. Umar, who was the same age as Abdullah, was his complete opposite; a typical city schoolboy who enjoyed video games and socialising.

The cousins greeted one another, but neither spoke. Seeing everyone together signalled the seriousness of the occasion. Their family had grown apart, with only brief encounters during Eid or at funerals.

Abbi inquired about Uncle Musa's job, "So, still at the library? Security guard, right?"

Uncle Musa nodded, "Yes, security guarding keeps me grounded despite the city's chaos. But times like these... they remind you of what truly matters."

Whispering quietly, Abdullah felt the weight of the day as he observed so many people, "Grandma's so loved."

Uncle Musa spoke to Abdullah gently, "And you are also blessed to be surrounded by so much love."

These words deeply touched Abdullah. It was a realisation that deepened by the recent loss of his beloved grandmother.

As Abbi and Uncle Musa continued to express their condolences to each other, Abdullah noticed everyone moving towards Grandma Jamila's body to carry her to the Masjid for the Janazah prayer.

"Time to pray," Grandpa Luqman said, standing ready.

Moments before the prayer began, Abdullah felt a rush of emotions inside him. Approaching Grandpa Luqman as his face radiated with wisdom, Abdullah asked, "How do you find strength in times like these, Grandpa?"

Grandpa Luqman placed a gentle hand on Abdullah's shoulder and replied, "My dear boy, we find strength in our faith and in knowing that the plan of Allah (The Most High) is perfect, even if we can't always understand it. We find strength in coming together as a family should, supporting one another. And most importantly, we find strength in our prayers and Dua, and in accepting the Qadr of Allah (The Most High). Never forget your identity. You are a Muslim, Allah (The Most High) is your Lord, and you are His slave."

The Janazah prayer was an emotional moment, with the family standing together in rows, facing the Qiblah, seeking the Mercy of Allah (The Most High) and His Forgiveness for the departed soul.

As Abdullah heard the Imam's voice reciting the Dua, the words echoed within him. He began to accept the finality of Grandma Jamila's passing and the changes it would bring to their family.

"O Allah, forgive our living and our dead, those present and those absent, our young and our old, our males and females."

After the prayer, Abdullah turned to Grandpa Luqman again and said, "Grandpa, it's so hard to say goodbye."

Hearing Abdullah, Ummi, who had been struggling to conceal her emotions, approached her grieving son. "We know it's hard, darling, but we're together in this," she said softly. "We will always make Dua for her."

Grandpa Luqman smiled and replied, "Indeed, my boy, it is. But remember, *with every hardship, there is ease. The Prophet Muhammad (peace and blessings be upon him) said, 'When a man dies, all his deeds come to an end, except for three: A continuous charity, knowledge by which people take benefit, and a pious son who prays for him.'* So, let your Grandma Jamila's legacy inspire you to be a better person every day, and ask Allah (The Most High) for His Mercy, and to allow us to unite in Paradise, insha'Allah. Now, let's go fulfil your grandma's rights," Grandpa Luqman stood up hastily.

As they walked towards the burial site, Abdullah felt a renewed sense of strength and understanding. They lowered Grandma Jamila's body into the ground as Abdullah held onto Grandpa Luqman's words, finding comfort in his wisdom.

The Janazah concluded, and everyone exchanged their condolences with one another before departing. Some offered to drop off food later that day for Grandpa Luqman. It was an overwhelming experience, both sad and beautiful at the same time, witnessing the strength and unity. It was indeed a bittersweet moment.

Abdullah, Grandpa Luqman, Abbi, Ummi, and little Ramlah embraced one another for what seemed like forever. It was a profound moment of unity that they wouldn't soon forget. And despite all their differences, they had one very important thing in common, their love for the Quran and Sunnah, and one another.

The summer sun continued to shine brightly overhead, a reminder that life carried on, and they would find the strength to move forwards together, from the teachings of the Quran and Sunnah with the understanding of the Salaf, as taught through Grandpa Luqman's wisdom.

Chapter 5: Hearts United

As the Hakeem family settled back at home, the gloomy atmosphere remained after Grandma Jamila's passing, and Abdullah and Ramlah found themselves coping in different ways.

Abdullah still yearned for his space and quiet moments of reflection to process his grief as he battled with the loss. In contrast, Ramlah, in her innocence, tried to reach out to her big brother, wanting to play and share moments of joy. However, her timing was unsuitable, as she approached him during his moments of solitude.

In the quiet of the afternoon, Abdullah stood beneath the garden tree, his thoughts lost in the day's events. Meanwhile, Ramlah's laughter and the repetitive thud of her ball against the tree's trunk broke the silence, testing Abdullah's patience.

"Careful, Ramlah! You're near the bees' home," Abdullah gently warned, concern in his voice.

"But it's more fun here. The tree's like my goalpost!" Ramlah cheerfully replied, her voice filled with innocence, unaware of the harm she was causing.

"That tree, and the bees it shelters, are important to us and the environment. Disturbing their home could harm them. Besides, I'm trying to sit here in peace," Abdullah explained, feeling a little frustrated.

"But I'm bored. Where will I play?" Ramlah questioned.

"It's not just about play. Bees are important; they pollinate our food. We need to protect them, as Grandma taught us about respecting all creatures," Abdullah replied, echoing their grandmother's wisdom.

An awkward silence fell between them as tension began to build, until Abbi arrived and intervened. "Is everything okay here?" he asked, his voice calm.

"I want to play, but Abdullah says it's dangerous for the bees." Ramlah explained, seeking validation.

"She was playing too close to the beehive," Abdullah pointed out, concern in his voice.

Abbi nodded, understanding both sides. "It's important for Ramlah to play safely. Hmm, the bees are vital too."

"See?!" Abdullah exclaimed, feeling supported.

Ramlah looked at them, seeking a solution, "So, what now? I don't want to sit and worry about bugs all day."

"Argh! They're not just bugs!" Abdullah declared, clearly frustrated, "I told you. It's about respecting nature."

"Well, let's find a balance." Abbi suggested, "It's about living together with nature, not disturbing it. Remember, Abdullah, you were just as playful as Ramlah is now when you were her age."

Ramlah apologised, feeling the guilt, "I didn't mean to make trouble."

"Thanks, Ramlah. We can still have fun without hurting the bees," Abdullah said, his voice softening. "We'll figure something out, insha'Allah."

Later that day, as Abdullah cuddled with Miza, Ramlah was on the other side of the living room floor playing alone, while Abbi attending to some paperwork in the corner. Ummi saw an opportunity to strengthen the bond between her children. Sensing the divide between them, she gently brought them together, encouraging them to express their feelings openly.

"Abdullah," Ummi began, her voice gentle yet firm, "I've noticed that you and Ramlah have different ways of dealing with Grandma's passing."

Abdullah watched his little sister, with a doll in her hand, and phonics book about bees teaching the 'ee' sound. She was ready to play at a moment's notice. He nodded with a pang of guilt, accepting their different ways of grieving. Miza trotted over and curled up next to Ramlah, joining her play.

Ummi continued, "You see, Ramlah finds comfort in play, and that's her way of coping. And Abdullah, I know you need your space to process your feelings. You're allowed to express grief in your own personal way as long as it doesn't harm anyone."

Abdullah glanced at Ramlah again, a newfound understanding beginning in his mind. He realised that he didn't have to bear the burden of his emotions alone. "And you know," Ummi said, smiling, "your differences can bring you closer together. Abdullah, you can explain to Ramlah when you need some space, and—"

"I could invite her to play once I've had time to myself." Abdullah suggested, showing his understanding.

"Yes, exactly! This way, you'll support each other through the tough times," Ummi concluded with a smile.

Abdullah nodded in agreement, appreciating his mother's advice as Ramlah listened closely.

Ramlah agreed enthusiastically, "Really?" she said, her boredom giving way to excitement.

It was a profound moment and new beginning in their sibling relationship, one that would help them work through the challenges of life together, hand in hand.

And in that tender moment, they learned to embrace and accept each other's unique ways of navigating their grief, shaping a deeper understanding and a stronger bond as siblings.

And so, Abdullah extended his hand to Ramlah, inviting her to join him and their friends for a picnic in the garden later that afternoon.

His best friend, Yusuf, would be coming with his little sister, Maryam, accompanied by their parents. They planned to drop off some food and offer their condolences to Grandpa Luqman, who was taking a nap in Abdullah's bedroom.

Ramlah beamed and gladly accepted Abdullah's offer to join the picnic. He asked her to grab her favourite book and a toy, and together, they headed to the garden to read while waiting for their friends. Ramlah picked up her phonics book, with her doll, Laila, and a pair of old mini binoculars.

Under Abdullah's favourite tree, they dived into the pages, discovering fascinating facts about the buzzing creatures. Suddenly, Abdullah had a wave of concern, urging him to ensure everything was in good order. He glanced around his tree, where the beehive rested.

While checking the area around the beehive, Abdullah's keen eyes caught sight of unusual footprints pressed into the soil. They stood out, clearly different from the typical animal tracks he was used to seeing. He wore a questioning expression as he leaned in closer, his mind racing to understand their origin. It dawned on him that a mystery was unfolding before his very eyes.

"Ramlah, can I borrow your binoculars?" Abdullah quickly scanned the farm, looking for anything unusual.

Unexpectedly, Yusuf and his family arrived, followed by a few classmates and their families, each held a dish or item to help ease the Hakeem family's grief.

As soon as Ramlah spotted Maryam, her face lit up with excitement and they couldn't contain their giggles. They eagerly ran off, hand in hand, ready for an exciting playtime adventure.

Yusuf greeted Abdullah enthusiastically, "Assalamu Alaikum, Merhaba, Abdullah! What's that you're doing?" He handed Abdullah flowers as a gift for his family.

Abdullah looked up, surprised by the sudden gathering of friends. "Oh, Wa Alaikum Salam, Merhaba, bro!" He smiled gratefully, accepting the gift, "We were reading interesting facts about bees. Bees love flowers! Just like my grandma did." Everyone exchanged glances.

Breaking the brief silence, Yusuf chimed in, asking "Bees, huh? What's so interesting about them, bro?"

Abdullah explained, "Well, they kinda work together like a team, just like our family. And they're super important for our survival. My grandma loved honey, so I thought it'd be nice to learn about it in her memory."

As everyone gathered around, their attention engaged, their hearts swelled with empathy for the young boy who had just experienced such a profound loss.

Yusuf nodded, trying to understand the emotion behind Abdullah's words, "That's a nice way to remember her. You know, Allah (The Most High) mentions in the Quran that honey has healing properties. It's like nature's medicine."

Abdullah agreed, the words of the Quran triggered his curiosity, "Exactly! It's amazing how something as small as a bee can do something so huge for the world."

Looking at the hive, Abdullah noticed a few struggling bees. "Not again," he murmured, the memory of the previous struggler clear in his mind. The repetition felt too deliberate, too unnatural. Instinctively, he reached out towards the hive, and a bee landed gently on his skin. He gasped and froze. "Okaay?" he thought aloud.

Everyone watched nervously, witnessing Abdullah's bravery. Grandpa Luqman appeared with admiration, "You're quite a bee whisperer, my boy," he commented.

Flattered by the compliment, Abdullah, continued to move closer to the hive, focusing on the struggling bee that had chosen his hand as its perch. The air was thick with tension and the sweet scent of honey.

The soft hum of the colony began to envelope Abdullah's hand, and he could almost feel the hive's collective heartbeat of vibrations on his palms.

Suddenly, amidst the calm, another bee, feeling threatened by Abdullah's close distance, darted forward and stung him on the back of his hand.

36

The pain was sharp and immediate, like a hot needle pricking his skin. Abdullah yelped, a mixture of surprise and hurt flashing across his face as he instinctively pulled away.

"Ow!" Abdullah yelled, watching a small mark form. The bee, its duty fulfilled, fell to the ground, lifeless.

Grandpa Luqman, with years of experience evident on his face, hurried over, his steps quick but steady. "Let me see that, Abdullah," he said, concern in his voice.

The guests stepped back, their earlier admiration turning to worry. Abbi appeared, quickly observing the situation, then sprayed a bee smoker at the bees to calm them down, redirecting the guests' attention.

Noticing the puzzled glances, Yusuf voiced his concern, "Is Abdullah okay?"

As Grandpa Luqman inspected the sting, he smiled reassuringly. "First things first, let's get the stinger out," he instructed, using a small, flat piece of card from his pocket, he gently scraped the stinger away without squeezing more venom into the wound.

"Ouch!" Abdullah winced, pain flashing across his face. "That really stings," he managed to say.

Ramlah and Maryam gasped as they witnessed Abdullah in pain from the sting. Their eyes widened in horror, frozen for a second before calling out for Ummi.

Ramlah, her voice trembling with urgency, cried out, "Ummi, quick! Abdullah got stung by a bee! Please, come!" Her eyes searched for her mother, seeking her comfort and aid.

Ummi, with her quick arrival and merciful nature, rushed to Abdullah's side, applying a cold compress on his hand, reducing the swelling and pain, "They must've wanted these flowers," she noted.

The other mothers immediately gathered around Ramlah and Maryam, their expressions softening with concern as they comforted the frightened girls, assuring them Abdullah would be okay.

Abbi waited anxiously. "That's it! We're not letting you near the bees again, not without supervision. No more close encounters without us nearby," he declared, his protective instinct taking over.

Abdullah frowned, feeling a mix of emotions. The fear of being stung again battled with an increase sense of resilience. "B-but, Abbi, I'm fine. I can learn to handle them properly," he objected, wanting his independence.

Grandpa Luqman stood up, clearing his throat, "Pain is part of learning. But we must not let fear stop us from living," he said wisely, glancing between father and son.

"I'm not afraid," Abdullah asserted, more to convince himself. "I promise I'm okay, Abbi."

Abbi sighed, torn between his instinct to protect and the desire to see his son grow. "Okay, but only once I get you full protective gear," he commanded, the weight of his decision heavy in his heart.

Abdullah nodded, understanding the importance of safety yet eager to learn more. As the conversation shifted, he took the moment to satisfy his growing curiosity about the bees. Turning to Grandpa Luqman, he asked, "Grandpa, what does bee whisperer mean?"

Grandpa Luqman explained, "A bee whisperer is someone who observes bees, understands their language, and they understand you, and caring for their needs, much like you were doing, my boy." In that moment, Abdullah longed for the bees to trust him, now fully aware of the significance of his role.

The other kids began to join in the conversation, sharing their own interests and stories, along with their hopes and fears. Abdullah realised that while he valued his own space, connecting with others brought a different kind of fulfilment. He couldn't help but feel a deep sense of belonging.

As the evening sun warmed the garden. Abdullah and his family, along with their friends, gathered for an early dinner. The males had set up outdoors, while the females had taken shelter indoors, with each guest bringing a dish to ease the Hakeem family's grief.

As the guests mingled, Yusuf pulled Abdullah aside, sensing his friend's need for space amidst the crowd. "Hey. You cool with us here?" he asked thoughtfully.

Abdullah smiled reassuringly, "You're like family, bro. I'm glad you're here. But it's cool if you wana go—"

Before Abdullah could finish his sentence, Yusuf quickly halted him, grateful for his kindness and the close bond they shared, "Nah! I'm happy to be here."

During the gathering, Abdullah slipped into the kitchen to fetch some cups. There, he unexpectedly found his mother placing the flowers into a jug near the window. They exchanged glances, and in that moment, they shared a silence that spoke volumes, expressing their shared sorrow without the need for words.

Just as Abdullah turned to leave, his mother softly called his name. "Abdullah."

"Yes, Ummi?" Abdullah paused, the lingering ache of the bee sting serving as a silent reminder of his mother's love and protective care.

She looked at him with a sense of pride, clearly wanting to say more. Instead, she casually inquired, "Abdullah, enjoy the sun, my darling, and don't forget to apply sunscreen. We need to make sure that your skin is protected, okay?"

Abdullah paused for a moment, deeply touched by his mother's constant support. Then, with gratitude in his voice, he replied, "Ummi, I'm sorry for going near the bees. I don't know what I was thinking. I'll be careful insha'Allah. May Allah (The Most High) reward you with good for your patience with me."

Ummi smiled with understanding. "It's all part of learning, my dear. Just promise me you'll stay safe."

"I promise, Ummi," Abdullah reassured his mother. "Do you think Abbi meant it when he said I need protective gear and supervision near the bees?" he asked.

Ummi chuckled, "Your father cares deeply. Anyway, we can't afford new things just now, so don't worry."

With those words, he left the kitchen, returning to the picnic outside, where the bond of family and friends provided solace during this challenging time. The day not only highlighted the importance of unity and cooperation but also reflected the family's dedication to peacefully living together with nature, inspired by their grandmother's lasting wisdom.

Chapter 6:
Staying Up Late

As Abdullah completed his nightly Quran recitation, he lay back in bed and revisited his grandmother's note, pondering the deeper meaning behind her treasured words, *"A sweet legacy awaits you, patience is key."* But as he drifted towards sleep, a faint sound from the garden below caught his attention. A sudden, distressing racket of bleats and mehs arose from his goats. He rushed to the window, his heart racing, wondering if it was just a trick of the imagination.

Abbi entered the room, smiling warmly to say goodnight. Seeing Abdullah's distant look, he knocked gently and repeated his greetings.

Snapping back to the moment, Abdullah let out a sheepish laugh, asking, "Heh heh. Sorry, Abbi. I was just wondering, have you seen anything strange lately, you know, around the farm?"

"Like what, Habibi?" Abbi replied, his brows raised in concern, glancing back and forth between Abdullah and the window.

Hesitating, Abdullah glanced down at his healing sting, before he began to share his concerns. "I, um, heard a weird noise coming from the goats just now, and the beehives look like they've been fiddled with lately."

Abbi considered Abdullah's words, assuming he was still grieving over his grandmother. He then walked over to Abdullah, who was aimlessly staring outside.

As Abbi observed the dark garden view, he said reassuringly, "There's nothing to worry about, Habibi. You're safe here. Maybe you're just tired and need some rest. Ignore the goats and go to bed."

But Abdullah's determination to uncover the truth couldn't be crushed so easily. And so, he decided to stay up late that night, hiding behind the bushes near the beehive. In one hand, he clutched a torch, while in the other, he held a notepad ready to record any unusual activity, and around his neck hung Ramlah's old mini-sized binoculars.

As the stars twinkled overhead, he anxiously watched and waited, he could feel his heart pounding in his chest. Each rustle of leaves or distant sound seemed like a clue to the mystery he was determined to solve. The night was silent, besides the chirping of crickets and the gentle rustling of leaves in the breeze.

Abdullah suddenly felt a soft nudge against his arm. "Subhan Allah!" Startled, he turned to see his cat, Miza, appearing from nowhere, curiously sniffing around. "Meeoooww!" Miza couldn't resist a little meow, and Abdullah, taken by surprise, whispered, "Shush, Miza." It was as if the mischievous cat sensed his worry and decided to lend some furry comfort.

Abdullah's eyes were fixed on the beehive, his grip on the torch tightening as he kept his senses sharp. Just when he began to wonder if his imagination was playing tricks on him, a shadowy figure emerged from the darkness, lurking around his tree.

Abdullah's heart skipped a beat as he struggled to make out the shadow's features behind his glasses. Was it the mysterious beehive thief he had suspected?

The figure moved with an unnatural grace, their intentions shrouded in secrecy. Miza, startled by the intruder, perked her ears up, her wide green eyes locking onto the direction of the sound, then quickly ran to hide behind the bush.

As adrenaline ran through Abdullah's veins, he steadied himself. He knew he had to be cautious. Anxiously waiting in suspense, he observed carefully through the binoculars, ready to unveil the truth. But before he could react or make sense of the situation, the mysterious figure vanished into the night, leaving him with more questions than answers. It was clear that the mystery deepened, and Abdullah's determination to uncover the truth only grew stronger.

As Abdullah's left hand gripped the pen tightly, he hastily scribbled down the time and date. But when he glanced at his notes, his heart sank, realising he had smudged the ink into a spidery mess. Frustrated, he crumpled up the paper and tossed it into the nearby bush, deciding it was time to call it a night.

Suddenly, a voice whispered, "Give my binoculars!" Ramlah crept up behind Abdullah. Surprised, he asked why she was out late. Ramlah replied, "Same as you."

"Quick, let's go to bed," Abdullah urged. As Abdullah and Ramlah crept back to the house through the back door with the sneakiness of two detectives on a mission, the leaves clung to Abdullah's clothes as evidence of his late-night outdoor adventure.

He noticed a rather unusual atmosphere in the living room. His parents, usually the example of peace and unity, were seated there, their voices quiet but intense. They were engaged in a whispered argument.

Abdullah, anxious and confused, kept moving, tiptoeing quietly towards his room, while Ramlah had already retreated to hers.

Just as Abdullah was about to reach the top of the stairs, his footsteps betrayed him with a creak that echoed under his footstep. He froze as he heard a soft sigh behind him. It was Abbi, who quietly stood there.

Abdullah met Abbi's stern gaze. His voice was a mix of concern and irritation as he wondered why Abdullah was up so late, and why leaves clung to his clothing. "You have broken the rules, Abdullah," Abbi said firmly.

"Abbi, I—" Abdullah started, swallowing hard.

"You know, I was looking everywhere for you and your sister. I thought something terrible had happened," Abbi sighed. "I value your safety and trust. Being out late without supervision is dangerous," he warned.

Feeling the weight of his actions, Abdullah looked down in shame, "Abbi, I'm sorry. I was checking on the bees."

"Listen, Abdullah," Abbi paused, carefully selecting his words. "Your heart was in the right place wanting to protect the bees, but you risked your safety and Ramlah's. It's important to understand why rules exist—they're there to keep you safe," he explained, hoping to instil a sense of responsibility in his son. "As your father, my job is to protect you, guide you, and love you. Do you understand what I'm saying?"

Abdullah nodded. Still, his heart was racing from earlier. He hesitated but decided to share what he had witnessed. His tone grew concerned as he said, "Abbi, I saw someone outside, you know, around the beehives."

Abbi took a deep breath in, his anger tempered by his understanding of the family's recent loss. "Abdullah, you're grieving. Sometimes, our minds play tricks on us when we're going through difficult times."

But Abdullah remained steadfast. He pleaded Abbi to check it out for himself, to ensure the safety of their home. Abbi finally agreed. After a quick inspection of the farm, Abbi found nothing wrong, leaving Abdullah puzzled. Perhaps he did need some rest, he thought.

"Is everything alright?" Ummi appeared, surprised at Abdullah's late wakefulness.

"Five minutes, Aish," Abbi responded, "I'm giving our son important advice." Ummi nodded, stepping back.

"Abdullah," Abbi paused, "when I was your age, my father would say *'great things happen when the energy of the youth work together with the wisdom of the elders.'* I didn't get it then, but I do now. We're a team."

"I thought I was being brave and protective," Abdullah said softly. "We're still going camping, aren't we?"

"Abdullah, bravery isn't about endangering yourself or others," Abbi gently corrected, "Do the right thing at the right time in the right manner. That's wisdom."

Abdullah's regret was evident. Abbi decided to conclude with a gentle reminder, "You know, I don't want to, but if this happens again, we may have to reconsider our camping trip."

"You'd take away camping?" Abdullah asked, surprised, realising now that true courage included considering safety and responsibility.

"Camping is a privilege, not a right." Abbi said firmly. "Promise me you'll think of safety first, especially for Ramlah. Rest now. We'll talk tomorrow, insha'Allah."

"Safety first," Abdullah promised. As he set off to his room, his mind filled with questions, he couldn't help but feel a growing communication barrier between himself and his father, and he yearned for his understanding.

Ummi, always watchful and caring, quietly followed Abdullah to his room. She knew her son's determined nature, and while she admired his curiosity and thirst for answers, she also understood the importance of a good night's rest. She gently guided him to his bed, ensuring he was comfortable under the soft blankets.

As Abdullah lay down, his eyes still filled with the events of the night, Ummi began to recite verses from the Quran in her soothing voice. The melodious words, filled with profound meaning, washed over Abdullah like a gentle wave, soothing him into a sense of peace.

With each verse, the weight of the world lifted from his young shoulders, replaced by a sense of serenity and safety. Abdullah's eyelids grew heavy as the verses of the Quran embraced his weary soul.

His eyes closing while seeking reassurance, asking, "You believe me, don't you, Ummi?"

Ummi responded with a gentle smile, her warm eyes meeting his, as she sought to shift his focus and calm his restless mind.

Abdullah whispered his bedtime Dua as Ummi continued her recitation, until sleep overcame him, finding peace in the soothing words of the Quran.

Chapter 7:
The Supplications

During the peaceful summer days that followed Grandma Jamila's Janazah, the Hakeem family sought solace in the shade of their garden.

Grandpa Luqman had been spending more time than usual at Abdullah and his family's home since Grandma Jamila's passing. They provided one another invaluable support and guidance during this challenging time.

Abdullah made a promise to himself that he would prioritise rest and actively work on putting his troubled thoughts behind him.

As Grandpa Luqman was Abdullah's favourite person, he took it upon himself to teach Abdullah and Ramlah specific supplications and verses from the Quran and authentic Hadith. Together, they aimed to seek the Mercy of Allah (The Most High) and His Forgiveness for their beloved grandmother.

One sunny afternoon, as they sat beneath Abdullah's favourite tree, he asked, "Grandpa, what Dua should we recite for Grandma Jamila?"

Grandpa Luqman smiled warmly, leaning in closer to hear better. He began to teach his grandchildren, "When we visit your grandmother's grave, we should say: *'May peace be upon you, O people of this abode, O believers and Muslims. We'll be joining you shortly if Allah wills. We ask Allah for wellbeing for ourselves and for you all.'*"

As Abdullah listened carefully, repeating the words to commit them to memory, Ramlah, ever the curious one, chimed in with a question, "Grandpa, what do we say for the other Muslims in the ground?"

Grandpa Luqman smiled warmly and continued, "When we think of the Muslims buried in the ground, we say: *'O Allah, forgive them. O Allah, have mercy on them.'*"

The garden became a special space, where they exchanged knowledge and made deeper connections. The thought of the act of praying for the other souls in the nearby graveyard brought Abdullah comfort. As they recited these supplications together, he felt a sense of harmony remembering his grandmother, and said, "Grandma used to teach me to make Dua, and tell stories around the campfire. I regret not listening more."

Grandpa Luqman, always the wise teacher, spoke softly to Abdullah, "Remember, my boy, our faith teaches us the importance of patience, humility, and wisdom in times like these. We learn from our experiences and grow stronger through them. These supplications are not just words; they're our connection to Allah (The Most High) and His infinite Mercy."

Abdullah nodded, and asked, "Thanks Grandpa. Could you tell me more about wisdom?"

Grandpa Luqman replied thoughtfully, "My boy, like bees building a hive, wisdom means putting things where they belong from beginning to end to make sure progress is built upon a strong foundation."

Abdullah paused, trying to take in his grandpa's words, then turned to his sister and asked, "Ramlah, do you remember the foundations of Islam, and five pillars?"

Ramlah's eyes sparkled with excitement as she pondered the questions. With a shy grin, she began, "The foundations in Islam are, um, THREE! To know Allah, know the prophet and know our religion," then continuing confidently, she listed the pillars one by one, "We say there's only One God that deserves to be worshipped, Allah. We pray five times every day, fast in Ramadan, and give charity if we can, and, and..." Ramlah's voice trailed off, and her brows creased in deep thought as she tried to recall the last pillar.

Abdullah, noticing her struggle, offered a helpful clue, "Something people do when they visit a special place?"

Ramlah's face lit up as the clue triggered her memory, "Oh, I remember! To do Hajj if we can!" she exclaimed.

Abdullah gave her a high five, beaming with pride. "That's absolutely right, Ramlah! You're so clever."

Before quietly walking away, Grandpa Luqman advised, "With true belief, now focus on acting upon it."

Ramlah giggled and went to play with Miza who was pouncing on the leaves and shadows with excitement. "Bet ya can't catch me!" she playfully challenged.

Abdullah, fully embracing his little sister's playful dare, grinned widely and responded, "Oh yeah? Watch out, 'cause I'm a super-fast bee coming to get you. Run! BAAAAAAAZZZ!" He made a hilarious buzzing sound that caused Ramlah to burst into laughter and run even faster around Abdullah's favourite oak tree.

They chased each other around, laughter filling the air. Their shared faith and knowledge filled their hearts and uplifted their moods amidst their recent sorrow.

Abdullah gently lifted Ramlah onto the sturdy branch, then leaped up beside her, playfully poking her arm. "I got you!" he laughed. She poked him back, and they continued their playful back-and-forth, both grinning.

Then, gazing at the view ahead, Abdullah exclaimed, "Wow, Masha'Allah! Have you seen how cool Mr. Lucas's meadow looks?"

"What's a meadow, Bodi?" Ramlah asked.

"Look at it! It's a big field full of flowers where animals like to play, bees come to find nectar, and we can run around and have fun all day. And...Did you just call me 'Boe-dee'?" Abdullah chuckled, ruffling Ramlah's hair.

"Yeah, 'cause it's cute, like bees," she giggled, looking up at him with wide, innocent eyes.

"Thanks, Ramz. I'll call you that, or 'Beady Eyes'—cute like a bee!"

Ramlah nodded, and began to turn her newfound name for Abdullah into a catchy rhyme. "There's a Bodi in the tree, he said 'Hello' to meee. He is a funny bee."

"Great job, Ramz! Masha'Allah, your phonics practice is really paying off," Abdullah praised her efforts, smiling.

As Abdullah continued observing the beautiful farm, he saw Grandpa Luqman and Abbi engaged in a deep conversation. Though he couldn't grasp their words, the importance was clear. It mirrored the joy he shared with Ramlah. "Alhamdulillah for everything," he exhaled.

The summer days were the start of Abdullah's journey in embracing change and his family's company.

A gentle breeze blew through, carrying the delicious smell of Ummi's baking to Ramlah and Abdullah. As Ramlah decided to head back inside to join Ummi, Abdullah noticed Abbi waving him over, holding an envelope. Curious, Abdullah quickly approached.

"What's this, Abbi?" he asked.

Sounding concerned as he handed the envelope to Abdullah, Abbi replied, "We received this letter today from *'concerned neighbours,'* demanding they call pest control on our honeybees for being a nuisance."

"*...remove your bees or we will call pest control,*'" Abdullah read aloud, his voice tinged with confusion. He looked at Abbi and Grandpa Luqman, all sharing puzzled expressions.

"Why would someone want our bees gone so badly?" Abdullah wondered aloud. Reviewing the letter again, he suggested, "Abbi, we should call someone, like someone who's in charge of this stuff. Someone might be able to advise us."

Abbi, thinking hard, seemed unsure. "I don't know, Habibi. Maybe it would be easier just to remove the bees if they're causing this much trouble."

Shocked by the suggestion, Abdullah responded passionately, "But Abbi, Grandma Jamila taught us how important honeybees are, not just for us but for the whole planet. Allah (The Most High) teaches us to avoid harming and to help others, bees included. How would we feel if we were forced out of our home?"

"You make a strong point, my boy," Grandpa Luqman interjected, supporting Abdullah.

"Alright, let's see what the local council advises, insha'Allah," Abbi concluded and dialled the council.

After a tense wait, he got through. The council official explained, "Unless the bees are a health hazard, like causing allergies, no one has the right to demand their removal. They're crucial for the environment. We always encourage peaceful resolutions and community support first. And maybe consider relocating the beehive if necessary."

Relieved, they all appreciated the council's advice. "Alhamdulillah," Grandpa Luqman murmured. "It's always best to seek help from the right sources."

"Yes, Grandpa," Abdullah nodded, recalling a verse from Surah Al-Hujurat, "Allah (The Most High) teaches us to investigate the truth."

Just then, Ramlah came out with a tray of pancakes. "Look! Ummi let me drizzle the honey from our bees!"

Seeing the pancakes, Abdullah smiled broadly. "Let's enjoy these together, Ramz."

Abbi's worries faded as he looked at his children and the lush farm around them. Grandpa Luqman smiled proudly at Abbi, "This is a wonderful reminder of our duty to nature and each other. May Allah (The Most High) bless us all with the correct knowledge, understanding, and true action upon that."

"Ameen!" Abdullah and Ramlah shouted out in unison.

The family's connection to their land and its creatures deepened, affirming their commitment to live harmoniously with Allah's (The Most High) creation.

Chapter 8:
Changes and More Changes

A significant change was about to unfold in the Hakeem family's home. Grandpa Luqman, a pillar of strength and wisdom, found himself facing a difficult decision.

He had spent over five decades on the serene farm, a place filled with cherished memories and quiet reflection. However, now the time had come for him to leave the familiar behind and embark on a new journey.

After lunch, Grandpa Luqman approached Abbi with sadness in his eyes, saying, "I'll be going to visit your mother's grave, son. I'll be back later, insha'Allah."

Abbi nodded, his eyes mirroring his father's sadness and reflecting understanding. "Take your time, Baba. We'll be here, insha'Allah."

With that, Grandpa Luqman set off for his first visit to Grandma Jamila's resting place, seeking solace and a moment of reflection in the tranquil surroundings of her grave. With every step he took, he sincerely prayed to Allah (The Most High) for His Mercy upon her soul.

Ummi and Abbi quickly gathered everyone in the family into the living room to announce that they had reached an agreement to move Grandpa Luqman in with them.

"Yay! Let's have a tea party! Come, Bodi." Ramlah exclaimed with joy, scooping Miza up in her arms. She dashed off towards her room, her laughter trailing behind her, eager to celebrate their little joy together.

"Bodi?" Abbi and Ummi said together, grinning.

Abdullah's heart burst with excitement at the thought of having his favourite person close by every day, learning from him and sharing precious moments together.

Yet, there was a twist to this new arrangement. Abdullah was told that he would need to give up his room to accommodate his grandfather, which meant sharing a room with his little sister, Ramlah.

At first, Abdullah resisted this change, feeling a bit uneasy at the thought of giving up his personal space.

With a concerned look on his face, Abdullah turned to Abbi and asked, "Abbi, I really want to have my own space for my studies and alone time. But how can I do that when I have to share a room with Ramlah?"

Abbi knelt down beside Abdullah, understanding his need for space. His voice was gentle yet firm as he said, "Habibi, we know it's a big adjustment, but it's important for Grandpa Luqman to be near us, especially after Grandma Jamila's passing. He needs our support and companionship. Sharing a room with Ramlah might be temporary. We'll figure something out, and in the meantime, let's make the best of it, okay?"

Ummi chimed in, her eyes filled with empathy. "O my dear, you'll have so much time to spend with your grandpa, insha'Allah. Plus, think about how much fun you and Ramlah will have sharing a room."

Abdullah bit his lip, torn between his love for his grandfather and his desire for personal space. The room felt heavy and tense as he struggled to come to terms with this uncomfortable change.

Abdullah rushed to his room, stumbling on the creaky stairs that Abbi promised to repair. He paused, took a deep breath, and continued up the steps. Upon entering his room, waves of nostalgia washed over him. It was as if he was saying goodbye to an old friend, although he knew it was for a good cause. He scanned his room, absorbed the familiar sights, knowing he'd have to give it up to accommodate his grandfather.

Just as he was about to sigh at the thought of leaving behind his cherished space, he noticed a heart-warming scene as he looked towards Ramlah's bedroom. She was in her own world, playing innocently with Miza. She had dressed up the fluffy feline in a tiny costume, complete with a comically oversized hat.

Miza's attempt to walk around with her new outfit provided endless entertainment as she tried to shake off the 'intruder' on her back. "MOWOWW?" she protested.

Abdullah couldn't help but chuckle at the adorable sight. Ramlah's playful pranks were like a breath of fresh air, reminding him that sometimes, innocence and laughter were the best medicine. He decided to join her in the fun, his heart warming at the thought. He found himself increasingly enjoying his little sister's company, actively participating in her playful activities, something he couldn't have imagined just a few days earlier.

"Ramz," Abdullah said with a smile, "mind if I join in on the fun?" Ramlah's eyes sparkled with excitement, and she agreed without hesitation, taking Abdullah's hand. Together, they embarked on an imaginative adventure, as Miza, with an unusual outfit, led them on a delightful journey of creativity and fun.

They grinned together as Miza finally wriggled out of the comical hat, dashing downstairs into the garden.

Abdullah and Ramlah chased after her, laughter echoing through the air. Abbi and Ummi exchanged speechless looks, noting the sudden shift in Abdullah's behaviour. Despite his hidden pain, he was learning to embrace what he couldn't control.

They played together with excitement in the garden, Abdullah and Ramlah's laughter blending in with the clucks of chickens and bleats of goats. It seemed as though the farm animals were joining in to celebrate the news of Grandpa Luqman moving in too.

Ramlah requested Abdullah to lift her onto the tree branch. After gently placing her there, Abdullah hurried to check his beloved bees and honeycombs. To his dismay, he discovered more honeycombs missing, stirring a wave of frustration and concern within him that he struggled to suppress.

Perched on the branch, Ramlah watched Abdullah check the bees. "What ya doing, Bodi?" she inquired.

"Have you been playing near the beehives again?" Abdullah asked, concern in his voice.

"No!" Ramlah exclaimed. "It wasn't me," she asserted.

"Someone has." Abdullah noted, concerned.

Abdullah deeply cherished the honeycombs on his favourite tree because they held a special connection to his late Grandma Jamila. She had once told Abdullah a heart-warming story about how these particular bees had arrived on their farm. He sank into a deep memory.

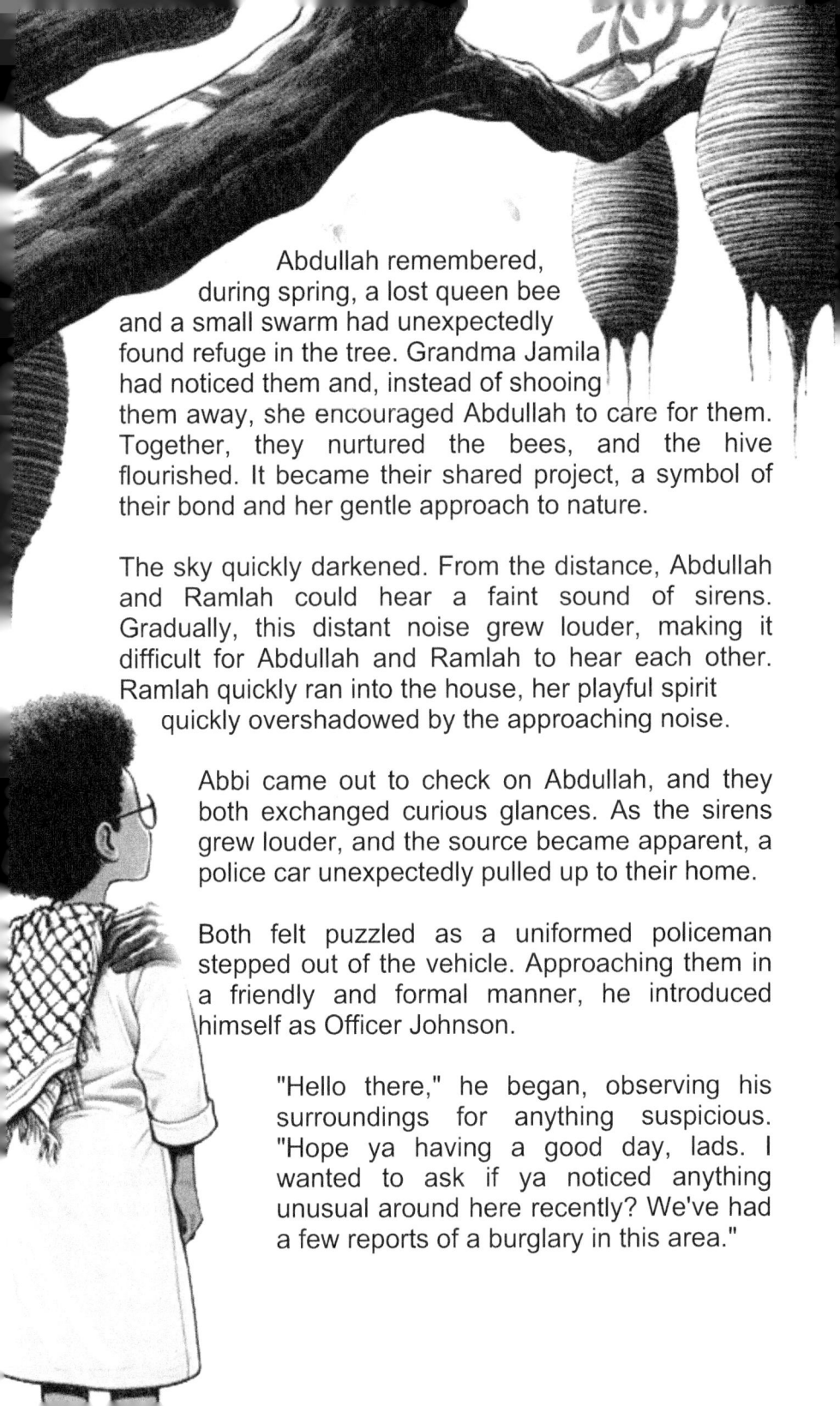

Abdullah remembered, during spring, a lost queen bee and a small swarm had unexpectedly found refuge in the tree. Grandma Jamila had noticed them and, instead of shooing them away, she encouraged Abdullah to care for them. Together, they nurtured the bees, and the hive flourished. It became their shared project, a symbol of their bond and her gentle approach to nature.

The sky quickly darkened. From the distance, Abdullah and Ramlah could hear a faint sound of sirens. Gradually, this distant noise grew louder, making it difficult for Abdullah and Ramlah to hear each other. Ramlah quickly ran into the house, her playful spirit quickly overshadowed by the approaching noise.

Abbi came out to check on Abdullah, and they both exchanged curious glances. As the sirens grew louder, and the source became apparent, a police car unexpectedly pulled up to their home.

Both felt puzzled as a uniformed policeman stepped out of the vehicle. Approaching them in a friendly and formal manner, he introduced himself as Officer Johnson.

"Hello there," he began, observing his surroundings for anything suspicious. "Hope ya having a good day, lads. I wanted to ask if ya noticed anything unusual around here recently? We've had a few reports of a burglary in this area."

Abbi glanced at Abdullah, who swallowed nervously before shaking his head. "No, Officer, we haven't seen anything," Abbi replied, observing his son's anxiety.

The policeman smiled warmly, patting Abdullah on the back. Meanwhile, another policeman spoke to Patrick Lucas, their neighbour, exchanging a few words before arresting him. Abbi advised Abdullah to go inside and inform his mother, and he quickly complied.

"Okay, thanks for ya help, lads," Officer Johnson said. "Please don't hesitate to report anything suspicious. We're here to keep the neighbourhood safe."

As Officer Johnson left, Abdullah and Abbi exchanged a confused look through the kitchen window, now tinged with both curiosity and uneasiness.

The unexpected visit had disrupted their playful moment, leaving them to wonder about the burglary and how it might affect their peaceful neighbourhood. Meanwhile, Abbi advised his family to be cautious, lock up, and remain alert.

Unable to hold himself back any longer, Abdullah blurted out, "Mr. Lucas is a burglar, isn't he?"

With concern, Abbi advised Abdullah to be calm and let the police handle it, saying, *"The Prophet Muhammad (peace and blessings be upon him) said 'Beware of suspicion, for suspicion is the worst of false tales.'"*

Abdullah was still convinced that he had indeed seen someone a few nights ago, and he struggled to accept that it might have been his own neighbour. With full intention to protect the area, he decided to put up a big *'Do Not Touch'* sign near the bees' tree.

Chapter 9:
A Promise to Keep

As Abdullah struggled with the adjustments ahead, he couldn't help but recall the sadness that showed in his grandfather's eyes earlier. He sensed that this move was not an easy one for his grieving grandfather, and the thought weighed heavily on him.

As usual, Abdullah sought quiet time under his tree to reflect upon the many changes unfolding around him. Ramlah followed him, with Miza in her arms, to be nearby. He felt overwhelmed but remembered his grandfather's wise words that the plan of Allah (The Most High) is perfect even when we don't understand it.

Heading towards his tree, Abdullah noticed Abbi tirelessly digging the soil, usually a sign of his father's anger. Abdullah's brows raised with curiosity as he looked at his father with genuine concern.

Meanwhile, Ramlah joined Miza, both of them jumping around in the grass and among the flowers nearby, which had started to blossom.

Abdullah approached Abbi, eager to inquire about his activities, "Abbi, what are you doing? Why are you digging a big hole in the ground?" he asked.

Startled, Abbi carefully placed the spade down, and said, "Well Abdullah, there's something important I need to bury here," pausing as he gazed down at the object cradled in his arms. "It's Grandma Jamila's keepsake box," a reflective look in his eyes.

Abdullah, his mind racing ahead of him, assumed Abbi's digging might be connected to the beehive thief he thought he had seen several nights ago.

He hesitated for a moment before finally voicing his concern, "Abbi, does any of this have something to do with the beehive thief?"

Ramlah, while still within earshot, could hear everything being said but was more focused on playing with Miza.

Abbi paused, his expression a mix of frustration and understanding, then replied, "No, Abdullah, we've already talked about this. It's unrelated."

Abdullah felt a pang of guilt for bringing it up again and quickly apologised, "Sorry, Abbi. I just had to be sure."

Abbi gave Abdullah a reassuring smile, and said, "No need to apologise, Habibi. Let's just stay focused."

Abdullah, sensing the gravity of the situation, gently questioned further, "So, Grandma Jamila's keepsake box? Why are you burying it?"

Abbi, his gaze still fixed on the box, explained patiently, "You see, Habibi, Grandpa Luqman has been deeply affected by Grandma Jamila's passing." He took a deep breath, as if carrying the weight of their collective grief. "Everything reminds him of her, so it has been quite difficult for him to move forward."

Abdullah, looking confused, suggested to his father, "Maybe I could look after it, Abbi. I promise not to open it," he offered earnestly. Abbi knelt down beside the hole, barely making eye-contact with his son. His heart ached, remembering his mother, and her legacy.

"Actually, before your grandma passed, she asked me to keep this special box for you, thinking you'll benefit from it someday." Abbi noted, "But your grandpa wants to remove all the precious memories of her from our home to ease his pain." Abbi carefully lowered the box into the hole. "I'll bury it here in the garden so we know where to find it when the time's right."

Abdullah, moved by Abbi's words, replied. "That box is for me?" He approached the hole, glancing at the box, a mix of emotions in his eyes, and gently continued, "It kinda reminds me of the box Grandpa gave me years ago. It must be really hard for Grandpa. Well, if keeping Grandma Jamila's memories safe for the future is important then I'll wait, insha'Allah."

Abdullah dashed up to his room, quickly pulling out his grandmother's note from his pocket. He paced back and forth, pondering the connection to her keepsake box. Seeing his father bury the box near the beehive, reinforced the idea that his note contained something immensely valuable or significant, possibly a hidden message. Various ideas started going through his mind, yet he lacked enough information to draw a conclusion.

Feeling lost, Abdullah decided to focus on memorising the Quran verses for his presentation on bees until he stumbled upon a verse about death, and it quickly reminded him of how short life is. Emotions overflowed, as he took this as a sign from Allah (The Most High), and his thoughts drifted back to his grandmother.

He reminisced their cherished moments, appreciating his family's sacrifices, and realised that, despite Grandma Jamila's absence, he still had his grandfather. As a few hours passed, gradually, Abdullah began to accept the reality of change.

He realised that giving up his room to his grandfather didn't mean losing his personal space. Afterall, he still had his Tree of Solace. Together with his family, they worked hard to prepare a warm and welcoming space for Grandpa Luqman.

As the evening arrived, Ummi tucked Ramlah into bed. Ramlah asked, "Ummi, what's a beehive thief?"

"Where'd you hear that, sweetie?" Ummi chuckled.

Ramlah explained that she had overheard Abdullah and Abbi discussing it earlier. Ummi clarified that a beehive thief is someone who steals beehives, honeycombs, or honey, but reassured her that there was no beehive thief here. As Ummi continued to speak, Ramlah gradually drifted into a deeper sleep.

Suddenly, the doorbell rang, announcing Grandpa Luqman's return from the graveyard. Ummi and Abbi rushed to the door to greet him. As Ummi offered a glass of water, Abbi insisted, "Please, Baba, stay a while. You look tired from all that walking."

Grandpa Luqman appreciated their warm welcome but gently replied, "May Allah (The Most High) bless you all, but I must be on my way. I just came to greet you since my home is just past the street from you. And there's one last thing I need to do." Abbi nodded with empathy, recognising the gravity in his father's eyes.

Abbi continued to insist that he at least accompany his father home. Abdullah chimed in, "I'll come with you too, Grandpa." He turned to his parents, seeking their permission, "Please?" They both exchanged agreeing glances with Grandpa Luqman, and off they walked together, three generations, side by side.

Chapter 10:
Time to Bid Farewell

It was time for Grandpa Luqman to bid farewell and set out on a new journey.

The next morning, as he sipped his tea in the small kitchen, he gazed at the empty chair across from him, which used to be occupied by Grandma Jamila. The pain of her loss still ached his heart, but he knew that he had to find a way to carry on without her.

After the passing of Grandma Jamila, Grandpa Luqman had been living alone on the farm. The farmhouse, once filled with the laughter and warmth of their family, had become a place of isolation and sorrow for him. The memories of his beloved wife echoed in every corner, and each passing day was a reminder of her absence.

Over the days that followed, Grandpa Luqman slowly began the process of letting go. He realised that the farm, once thriving with life and productivity, had become too much for him to manage alone. The upkeep of the land, the care of the animals, and the daily chores had become physically and mentally demanding, and he often found himself exhausted.

One day, Abdullah visited Grandpa Luqman at his farmhouse, sensing the weight of his struggles. Everyone awaited his arrival, but he hesitated. Abdullah sought uplifting words as they sat under the shade of a tree, and Grandpa Luqman finally shared his feelings with his caring grandson.

"Abdullah, my boy, I want to thank you for all your help on the farm lately," Grandpa Luqman said, gifting a few coins as pocket money. "It's not much, but perhaps enough for a treat, maybe some ice cream."

Abdullah accepted with a grateful smile, "Oh, thanks, Grandpa! You really didn't have to."

Grandpa Luqman's eyes twinkled, "Your visits brighten my days, young man. May Allah (The Most High) bless you with good for your kind heart."

Abdullah, humbled, replied, "O Grandpa, I enjoy being here with you."

Grandpa Luqman, overlooking the farm, added, "You know, when I was your age, I always believed in living a simple and humble life. When I married your dear grandmother, we promised to follow the example of the Prophets (peace and blessings be upon them all) and we never wanted to leave behind wealth or belongings. And now, with her gone, I realise it's time to let go, to pass on what we have to those who can benefit from it."

Abdullah listened, his heart heavy with empathy for his grandfather. Somehow, he knew that this decision had not come easily to his grandfather, who had spent most of his life working the land. The idea of leaving the farm, a place filled with cherished memories, was a profound and emotional one.

"Grandpa," Abdullah said in a comforting tone, "it's okay to let go. Grandma Jamila will always be in our Duas. And you've shown me that helping others is a good thing. By giving to those in need, you're carrying on her legacy of kindness and giving. Grandma once told me Surah Takathur teaches us not to pile up worldly stuff."

Proud of Abdullah's growth, Grandpa Luqman replied, "You're right, my boy. I'm letting go of the farm but holding onto its memories. It's time to pack. Oh, and the plural of 'Dua' is 'Ad'iya', not Duas—it's an Arabic word," he added, gently correcting him with a smile.

And so, the process of transition began. Grandpa Luqman started by giving away some of the farm's produce to neighbours and friends, just as Grandma Jamila would have wanted. The rest was donated to local charities, ensuring that nothing went to waste. Then, he handed Abdullah the last box to sort through.

While sifting through his grandmother's belongings, Abdullah discovered a note similar to the one Grandpa Luqman handed him at the funeral. He wondered if there was any connection. It read:

"Seek aid under the old oak tree."

Grandpa Luqman, puzzled, took the note. "Your grandma was full of surprises," he said. Abdullah wondered what his grandmother was trying to convey yet he remained silent, respecting his grandfather's moment and hoping to solve the mystery himself.

Time passed, and whatever remained was sold from their little wealth to pay for the month's bills. It was a bittersweet moment, as he knew he was honouring his wife's requests, yet it also marked the end of an era.

With his farm and possessions passed on to those who will continue its legacy of hard work, Grandpa Luqman made the difficult decision to leave the farmhouse behind. It was a place where he and Grandma Jamila had built a life together, but he knew that he couldn't stay there without her.

And although the Hakeem family lived only minutes away, Abbi arrived just in time to offer his father a helping hand with packing his belongings. Grandpa Luqman's farewell concluded as he handed the house keys to his landlord.

Upon returning home, the Hakeems noticed a new family moving into the house once occupied by Mr. Lucas. This triggered Abdullah's curiosity, pushing him to introduce himself to the newcomers. Abbi engaged in a short and friendly conversation with the head of the household, Aiden. Meanwhile, his wife, Margaret, nudged their son, Tony, urging him to greet Abdullah. Tony, about Abdullah's age, seemed disinterested, leaving Abdullah with an unsettling feeling.

Later, the day took another turn when Abbi, while trimming the bushes, found a crumpled-up note Abdullah had tossed away a few days earlier, including a specific date and time. Concerned, Abbi prompted a father-son conversation that had been overdue.

"Abdullah," Abbi began, his brow raised, "what does this note mean? The date matches the night you said you saw something when you stayed out late. Can you recall what you saw?"

Abdullah hesitated but decided to share his memories. "I thought I saw someone. It was a shadow, Abbi, but not clear. But it was definitely there. I tried to tell you."

Abbi's eyes widened. Could Abdullah's sighting be an alibi for Mr. Lucas? If Mr. Lucas was in the farm at the time of the burglary, perhaps he wasn't the burglar. "But what was Mr. Lucas doing lurking around our farm?" Abdullah wondered. The mystery deepened, and his mind was filled with questions and possibilities.

Chapter 11:
Learning from Grandpa Luqman

Over the days that followed, the change in Grandpa Luqman's living arrangements had settled comfortably. Abdullah found himself sharing precious moments with his grandfather during the long, hot summer afternoons.

As Abdullah sat with Grandpa Luqman under the tree's shade, gazing at the golden fields, they enjoyed a generous portion of dates and a glass of fresh raw milk from the farm. Meanwhile, Miza entertained them by pouncing on any small insect that dared to enter her view. This playful scene triggered Abdullah to climb the tree and inspect the beehives. There, he discovered new signs of tampering, and it looked intentional.

Careful not to jump to conclusions, Abdullah drew his attention back to his grandfather. "Grandpa, the stories about your younger days are so inspiring," he said, casually hanging from a tree branch with one hand.

Grandpa Luqman turned to his grandson, a note of pride in his voice, and said, "Ah, Abdullah, stories are very powerful, you know. They teach us important lessons about life, patience, gratitude, and kindness. And I must say, seeing you hang on to that tree branch with just one hand, my boy, you've got strength and determination. You'd make a fine farmer someday."

Abdullah jumped down from the tree, dusted his hands, and blushed. "Like the story of how you turned an empty piece of land into a successful farm, even after years of hardship? That must've been tough, Grandpa."

Grandpa Luqman chuckled softly. "Indeed, it was, my boy. I faced hardship, but I also learned the value of hard work and patience. Life isn't always easy, but it's those challenges that make us stronger."

Abdullah's eyes sparkled with curiosity. "And what about the story of the helping hand you received from your friendly farm neighbour during a difficult time?"

Grandpa Luqman's face softened as he recalled that distant memory. "Well, my boy, one time, I was faced with hardship, and a nearby farmer offered his support. It reminded me of the Sadaqah taught by the Prophet Muhammad (peace and blessings be upon him) and his companions (may Allah be pleased with them all). It truly inspired me to help others in need too."

Abdullah leaned in, absorbed in his grandfather's stories. "That's amazing, Grandpa. I want to be like that, too, helping others when they need it."

Grandpa Luqman's heart swelled with pride and joy. "You already are, Abdullah. I've seen how kind and caring you are with Ramlah and how you help your family. Remember, Sadaqah applies to all good deeds, and is like a treasure that multiplies when shared."

During their conversation, Ramlah popped up, holding her doll Laila, and nestled near Grandpa Luqman.

Grandpa Luqman began to tell another story, Abdullah and Ramlah leaned in. "Ah, allow me to tell you a story about kindness and sharing. It's about your Grandma Jamila's big dream. She was an amazing woman with a big heart. She dreamt of returning to her homeland and starting a big honey-making business, one so big that she could give honey away for free to those in need."

As Grandpa Luqman shared their story, Abdullah and Ramlah were captivated by every word. The story was filled with Grandma Jamila's research on honey's healing properties and her dreams of helping others.

As soon as Grandpa Luqman mentioned the word 'bees,' Ramlah's ears perked up, and her excitement bubbled over. She couldn't contain her suspicion any longer. "Abdullah," she blurted out, interrupting the story, "do you take honeycombs from the beehives?"

Abdullah was taken aback by Ramlah's false suspicion, experiencing a mix of frustration and sadness. He whispered to Grandpa Luqman, attempting to clear his name, "I don't, Grandpa. I promise."

Leaning in, Grandpa Luqman tried to intervene. "Now, let's not jump to conclusions, Ramlah. Blaming someone can hurt feelings. Abdullah is a kind and honest boy. We should discuss this calmly."

Ramlah looked in Abdullah's direction unsure and said, "But why would Ummi and Abbi say he did?"

With wide eyes, Abdullah gasped, "Abbi and Ummi said what?!" His sister's words took him by surprise.

At that moment, Abbi walked in and overheard their conversation. He approached them, shaking his head with a soft smile. "Sweetie, that's not what we said. Abdullah is innocent. Let's choose our words carefully."

Ramlah looked at Abdullah with her adorably big eyes, understanding her father's words. "Sorry, Bodi."

"Misunderstandings happen sometimes, you know." Abbi gently reminded them, "Let's all learn from this."

Then suddenly, the doorbell rang, and Abbi's eyes widened in excitement. "Oh, that must be my new laptop!" he exclaimed as he headed towards the door.

Abdullah was taken aback. "Laptop?" he asked.

Abbi, on the other hand, wasn't finished yet. "Oh, and what's that earbud thing Miza's playing with?"

Confusion deepened on Abdullah's face. "Earbuds?" he mumbled. "But I don't have—" Before he could finish his sentence, Abbi hurried off to answer the door, leaving Abdullah in a state of wonder. He rushed to inspect the earbuds Miza had been toying with, only to discover it was a hearing aid piece with a note attached to it. He recognised the handwriting immediately, his grandmas,

"Follow the trail where flowers bloom."

Abdullah wondered why a note was attached to a hearing aid. He knew only Mr. Lucas and his grandfather had slight hearing impairments. In that moment, something struck Abdullah, and he yearned to confront Mr. Lucas about his missing honeycombs.

Grandpa Luqman, with his patience, resumed the story. But then, as he reached an important point, his voice trailed off. He struggled to recall what happened next. Abdullah's early excitement faded into disappointment as an awkward silence settled in.

Sensing his grandfather's distress, Abdullah, with his youthful wisdom, smiled. "Grandpa," he said, "it's okay. Sometimes we forget things. Maybe you can tell me the rest of the story next time. I still loved hearing about Grandma's dreams and your adventures together."

Grandpa Luqman's eyes brightened with gratitude as he said, "You're right, my boy. Memory may fade, but the love and support of our family remain constant."

The disappointment melted away, replaced by a warm sense of togetherness as they continued to enjoy the evening by the farm. Grandpa Luqman began talking about the value of honesty and how telling the truth should be a guiding principle in one's life.

"Abdullah, my boy, remember that honesty is like hot coal. It may be difficult to uphold at times, but it shines brightly and is always worth it. Ah, *the Hadith about hot coal* comes to mind," he stated.

"H-hot coal?" Abdullah stammered, feeling sweaty as he remembered the hidden keepsake box, a secret he had yet to share with anyone. Keeping a secret from his beloved grandfather made him very uncomfortable.

Grandpa Luqman noticed Abdullah's uneasiness, but he assumed he was tired. He smiled at Abdullah and changed the subject. "Abdullah, do you remember when we used to dig together on the farm? You were just a little boy. Always so curious and adventurous. You are quiet these days."

Abdullah scratched his head, the memories felt distant. "Yes, Grandpa, I remember. Well, kinda remember."

Grandpa Luqman, recalling the past, offered, "If you want to learn gardening, my boy, just ask me anytime."

Nodding respectfully, Abdullah felt a sudden knot in his stomach at the mention of digging. His thoughts turned to the keepsake box again. Grandpa Luqman raised an eyebrow, sensing the change in Abdullah's mood.

"Abdullah, are you okay, my boy?" he asked. Before Abdullah could reply, the doorbell rang. Ummi called him to answer the door. Grandpa Luqman, ready for his afternoon nap, encouraged him to go.

As Abdullah dashed to open the front door, Yusuf greeted him with a curious glance. "What's up? You look troubled," Yusuf said, stepping inside.

Seizing the moment, Abdullah confided in Yusuf about the beehive thief, detailing everything he knew. "Quick, come this way," he urged, leading Yusuf to the garden. "Grandma left notes, honeycombs are missing, Mr. Lucas was arrested and moved, and Abbi buried something. I think it's all connected to the bees."

"Let's check it out," Yusuf suggested, eager to take action, and help his best friend solve a mystery.

Discovering a trail of flowers near his tree, Abdullah exclaimed, "Look! Someone's been stealing them!"

"Wait, these flowers, they're leading somewhere," Yusuf observed. "Didn't your grandma mention a trail in her note?" The trail led them to the wildflower meadow, previously owned by Mr. Lucas.

"Where exactly does this lead?" Abdullah wondered. "And who left this trail if Mr. Lucas moved?" he added.

Just then, an answer felt close, but their search came to a halt when Abbi called, "Boys, time for Maghrib!"

As Abdullah and Yusuf prepared to leave, they caught Tony staring sternly from his window, unsure of how long he'd been watching. "Who's that?" Yusuf wondered. "New neighbours," Abdullah responded.

Chapter 12:
Grandpa Luqman's Acceptance

As the summer days passed, Grandpa Luqman's sadness about leaving the farm slowly faded away. He had become a very important part of Abdullah, Ramlah, and their parents' lives. Ummi and Abbi often thanked him for the wisdom he brought into their home.

Summer nights meant storytelling under the starry sky. Grandpa Luqman shared tales from his youth, teaching valuable lessons. Abdullah, Ramlah, and their parents listened closely.

One starry night on the bench, Ummi turned to Abdullah, saying, "Having Grandpa Luqman with us has been a blessing. His wisdom enriches our lives."

Abdullah agreed, noticing how his grandfather showed wisdom not just in words but in his actions. His calm patience, kindness, and never-ending quest for knowledge left a deep impression.

Despite his age, Grandpa Luqman found the strength to do manual work again. He worked hard around the farm, teaching the Hakeem family to fix things instead of replacing them. He even lent a hand to Abbi in fixing the squeaky stairs as Abdullah observed closely. Grandpa Luqman's humility and commitment inspired the whole family, showing wisdom was a way of life.

That evening, Abbi asked Abdullah about his future. "Abdullah, have you ever thought about what you want to be when you grow up, insha'Allah?"

Abdullah thought for a moment then replied, "I want to be like Grandpa Luqman when I grow up – wise, patient, and always ready to help. I want to explore and travel, like adventurers who discover new things. Maybe I'll work on the farm, or study the Quran and authentic Hadith and teach others, insha'Allah."

Abbi and Ummi were pleasantly surprised, while Grandpa Luqman looked humbled saying, "How wonderful! May Allah (The Most High) bless you, my boy. You know, your grandma loved to help others in their time of need. She always went that extra mile to hide extra surprises too. It was like finding a treasure within a treasure."

Abdullah's excitement got the better of him. In a hushed voice, he said, "Abbi, maybe there's treasure in grandma's box—" referring to the buried keepsake box.

Diverting the subject, Ummi cut in and asked, "And how's your homework about bees going, Abdullah?"

With the mention of his favourite animal, Abdullah's attention was drawn to his mother, "It's cool, Ummi. I was going to work with grandma on it. She left me some references. I've been spending more time watching our bees. They're like a little family, like us. They work really hard, and guess what? They talk by wiggling! It's like their secret code. I've learned loads. Can't wait to share it in my presentation, insha'Allah."

Everyone looked impressed by Abdullah's newfound knowledge and enthusiastic interest in bees. Ummi smiled, replying, "Well, Grandma Jamila would've been so proud of you, my dear."

Yet, Abdullah turned to his father again, "Abbi I—"

Abbi sternly replied, "Not now, Abdullah," adding tension to the atmosphere. Abdullah's eyes widened as he noticed a bee gently land on top of Abbi's head. A moment of silence passed before Abdullah whispered, "Abbi, stay very still. There's a bee on your head."

Abbi froze, his earlier irritation fading into surprise. "What? On my head?" he whispered back in disbelief.

"It's okay, could be a worker or drone bee. Workers search for food and guard the hive; drones are male bees that can't sting," Abdullah explained, slightly nervous. After closely inspecting, he confirmed, "Oh. It's definitely a worker bee," his heart racing with the thrill of the challenge ahead, eager to impress his father.

Gently, Abdullah extended his hand, inviting the bee to crawl onto his perfumed-scented sleeve. Moments after, the bee landed onto his hand. A bead of sweat formed on his forehead, feeling the faint vibrations of the bee, a feeling he had grown to understand and love. "We're taking you back home," he murmured to the bee, a promise to both the bee and himself.

Abbi watched, stunned, as his son communicated with the bee. "How did you...?" he gasped, lost for words.

"It's what I've learned, Abbi. To listen, to understand," Abdullah replied, his eyes locked on the bee.

As they walked towards the hive, Abdullah leading with the bee in hand, Abbi couldn't help but feel a sense of pride. "They like your scent." Abdullah joked.

His son had not only mastered the art of beekeeping but had also formed a deep connection with the bees, a skill beyond his own. Relieved, Abbi lost track of earlier.

Still, Abdullah felt uneasy about hiding the keepsake box and was eager to confront it.

The family gathered in the living room where Ramlah had been playing with her toys on the floor nearby, blissfully unaware of the tension that entered the room.

Abdullah and Abbi exchanged glances, silently agreeing to tell Grandpa Luqman about the keepsake box. With a slight hesitation, Abdullah looked at Grandpa Luqman and said, "Grandpa, there's something we want to tell you."

Grandpa Luqman smiled, "Tell me what, my boy?"

Observing the innocence in his father's eyes, Abbi couldn't help but feel a sense of protectiveness. He quickly insisted, "Ahem... Actually, Abdullah, you can show me your homework on bees. Please excuse us."

Abbi and Abdullah left the room to find a quiet corner. Speaking softly, Abbi said "Abdullah, understand that we're not hiding the keepsake box to hurt Grandpa."

Abdullah looked puzzled, "But secrets are wrong—"

Abbi, with a firm yet gentle tone, whispered, " Abdullah, nobody is keeping secrets! We don't keep secrets or hide the truth. But some matters are private, like personal issues. It's important to let someone know if you believe something is harmful or uncomfortable. But this is about respect and trust." He took a deep breath in before continuing, "Your grandma requested this. She, like the Prophet's wife Khadijah (may Allah be pleased with her), knew her husband better than anybody. She was his biggest support. This is not easy for anyone, you know."

Abdullah scratched his forehead, his young mind trying to grasp the depth of his father's words. Abbi continued, "Look, one day you'll understand, insha'Allah. For now, trust Allah (The Most High). Do what's right."

After pondering, Abdullah nodded slowly, "I'm sorry, Abbi. I'll keep the box between us." Then, with an innocent look, he pleaded, "But can you at least tell me what's inside? Please? It's really hard for me."

"Okay," Abbi smiled, touched by Abdullah's plea. He took a deep breath in, showing hesitation but understanding, and agreed, "I'll reveal the box's contents. But I need time to think. Promise me this, you'll keep quiet for at least another week or two, and you won't bring it up again during that time, and NO more searching for a non-existent beehive thief. Deal?"

"Abbi, but I—" Abdullah started, feeling frustrated.

"That's my condition. No means no," Abbi interjected.

Abdullah bit his lip at the thought of abandoning his search for the beehive thief. "I promise, Abbi," he said reluctantly, nodding at his father in agreement.

Standing with a serious expression, Abbi remarked, "You know, you're quite mature for your age." His voice was steady yet filled with emotion as he continued, "Your grandma Jamila left a Will when she was alive. She made specific requests, and it's our duty to fear Allah (The Most High) and obey it."

Abdullah, sensing the weight of the conversation, hesitated before asking the question that had been playing on his mind. "Abbi… How did Grandma Jamila, you know, pass away?"

At first, Abbi found it difficult to speak, the words catching in his throat as memories flooded back. But with a deep breath, he shared, "Your grandma... she died from an allergic reaction to a bee sting. She had other underlying health issues, so by the time the ambulance arrived, it was too late."

The room fell silent, the only sound was the gentle ticking of the clock on the wall. "Grandpa Luqman and Grandma Jamila loved bees and honey," Abbi continued, a hint of warmth returning to his voice. "They knew so much about them. They shared a dream of starting a honey-making business that would be so successful, they could give honey away for free to the sick and needy."

Abdullah listened carefully. "Is that why you've been so protective?" he asked, suddenly beginning to understand the depth of his father's support.

"I care about you, Abdullah," Abbi sighed, "Plus Grandpa says he needs time to rethink if this is really something he wants to pursue."

"How will he know?" Abdullah asked quietly, trying to understand his grandfather's grief and hesitation.

Abbi looked up, lost for answers, "When he's ready," he said simply. "In matters of the heart and dreams, only Allah (The Most High) Knows. We must give him that time, Abdullah."

Abdullah nodded, taking in his father's words. He thought about his grandmother's Will, her love for bees, and her dream. It struck him then, the importance of legacy, of dreams passed down, and the resilience needed to carry them forward.

In that moment, Abdullah made a silent promise to himself. He would continue to learn everything he could about bees and honey, not just to honour his grandmother's memory but to keep the dream alive.

Looking over his glasses at Abdullah, Abbi inquired about his bee sting. "Has your sting healed yet?" his voice filled with a father's concern.

Abdullah grinned, and nodded, "Yes, Abbi, it's all better now, healed fast. Alhamdulillah. I'm not scared, you know," he replied, his eyes reflecting toughness.

"Alhamdulillah," Abbi responded, his expression softening. "Remember, bravery isn't about not feeling fear; it's about overcoming it. Just like you did."

Abbi's words had struck Abdullah's heart, challenging his perspective, "Jazakom Allahu khair for caring, Abbi."

As they both turned to head back to the living room, Abdullah paused and turned to Abbi. "Do you still want to see my homework, Abbi? I mean, well, it's not finished yet but—" he asked, with a glint in his eyes.

Abbi laughed and returned the playful grin, "Last one there is the king of the barn for a day!"

Abdullah playfully replied, "You're on!" With that, they raced up the sturdy, fixed stairs, laughing, eager to see Abdullah's unfinished bee-themed homework.

As the summer continued, the family grew closer, and Grandpa Luqman felt more at home. Each day brought new opportunities for growth, and Abdullah, although hesitant at times, blossomed under his grandfather's wisdom, mother's mercy, and father's protectiveness.

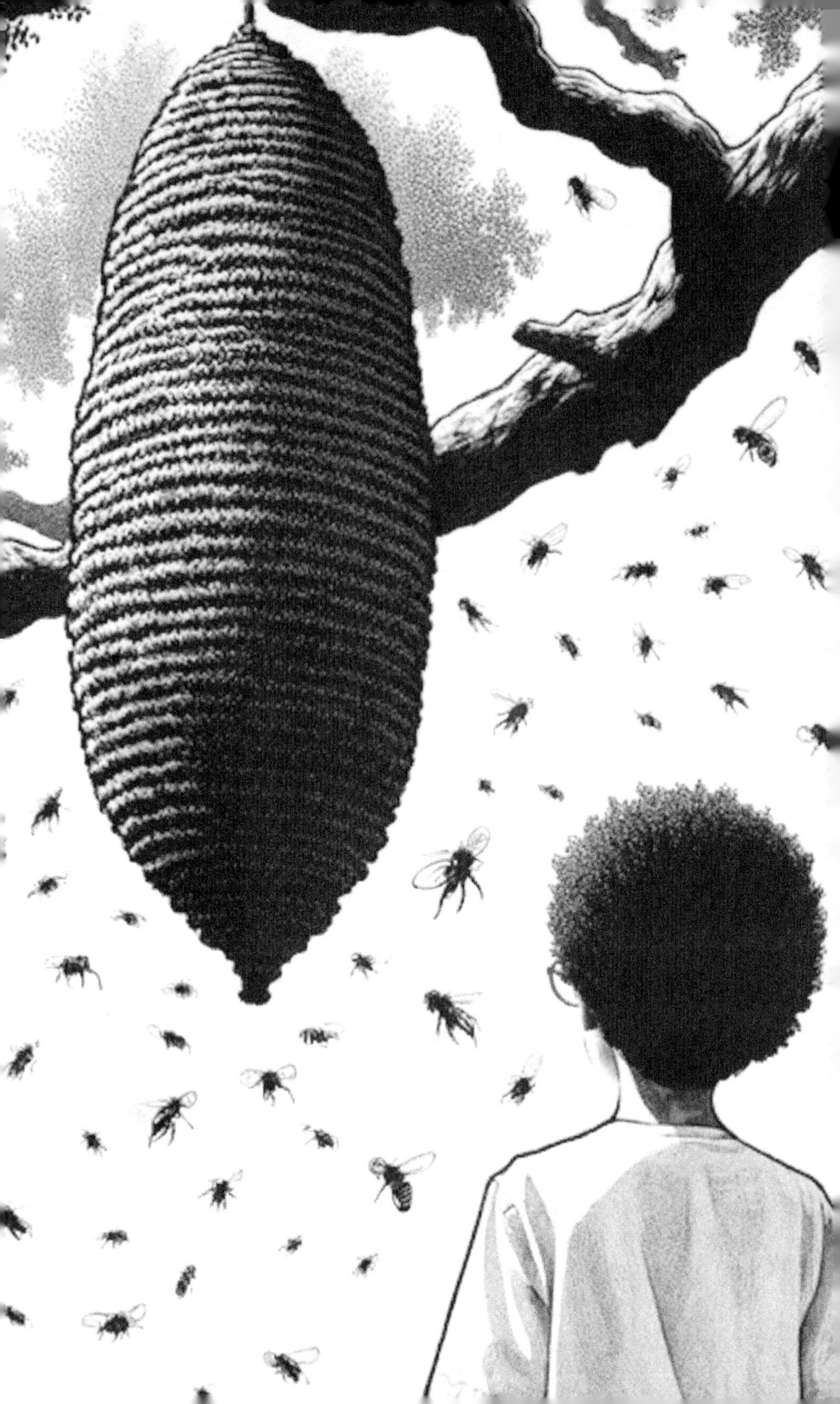

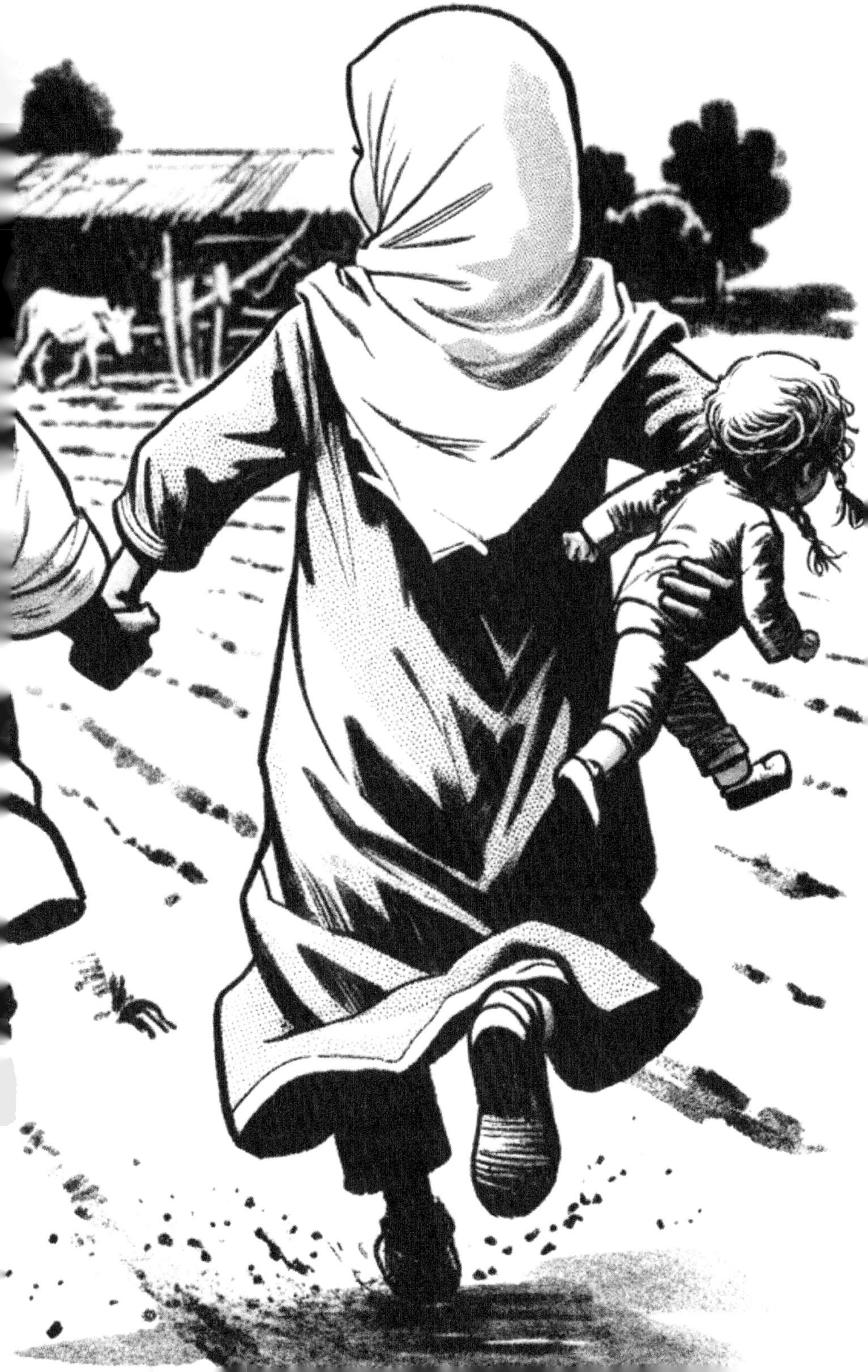

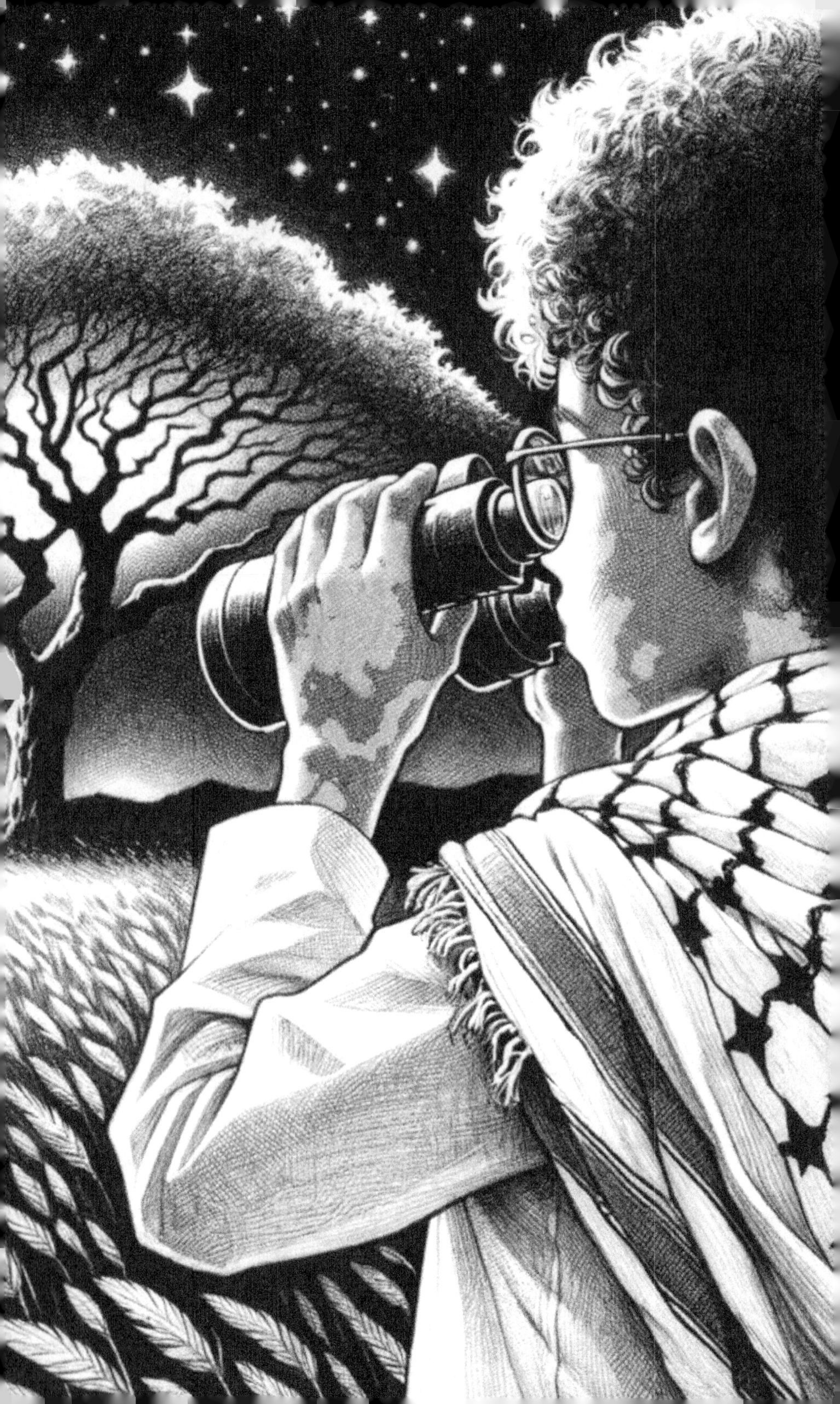

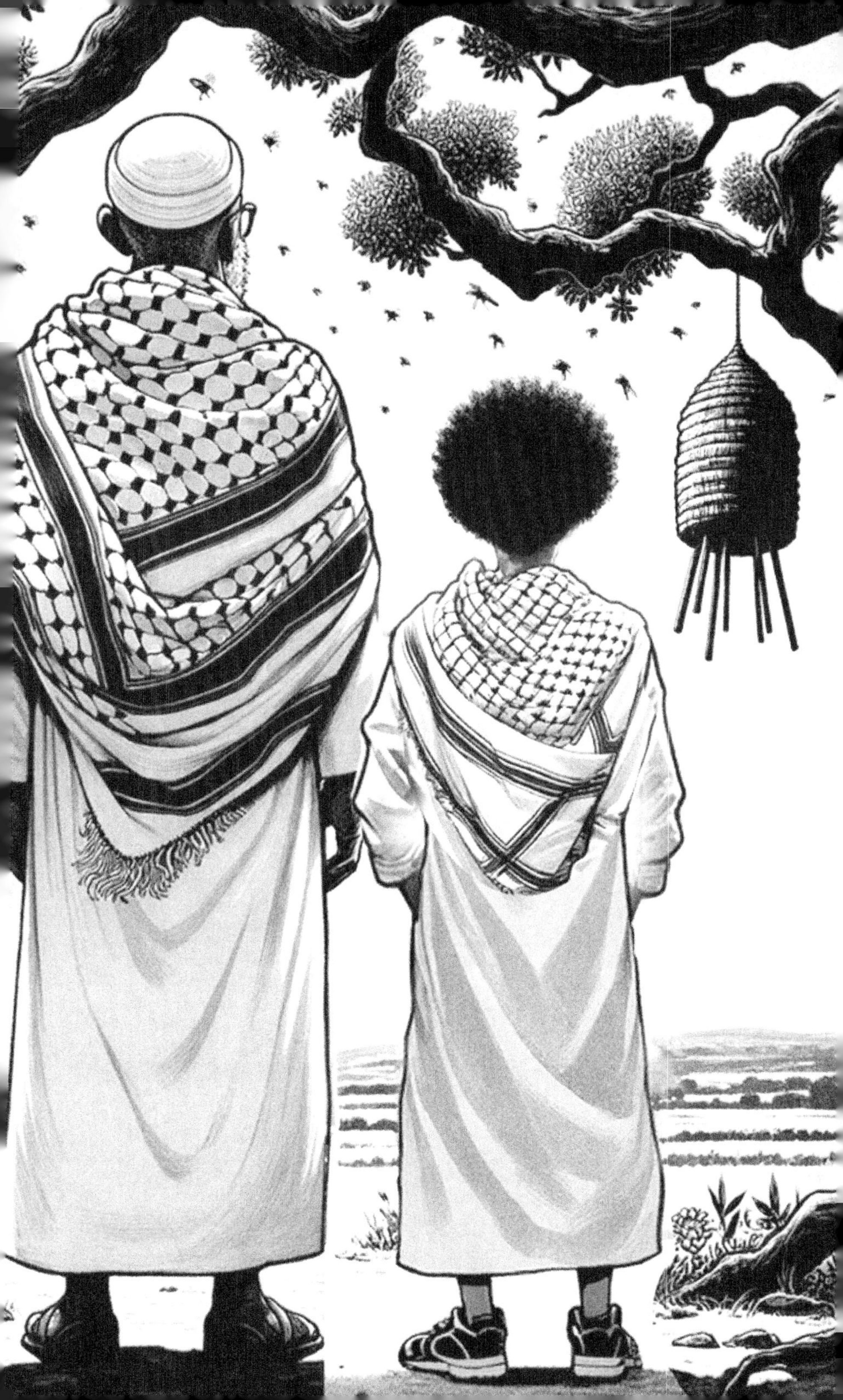

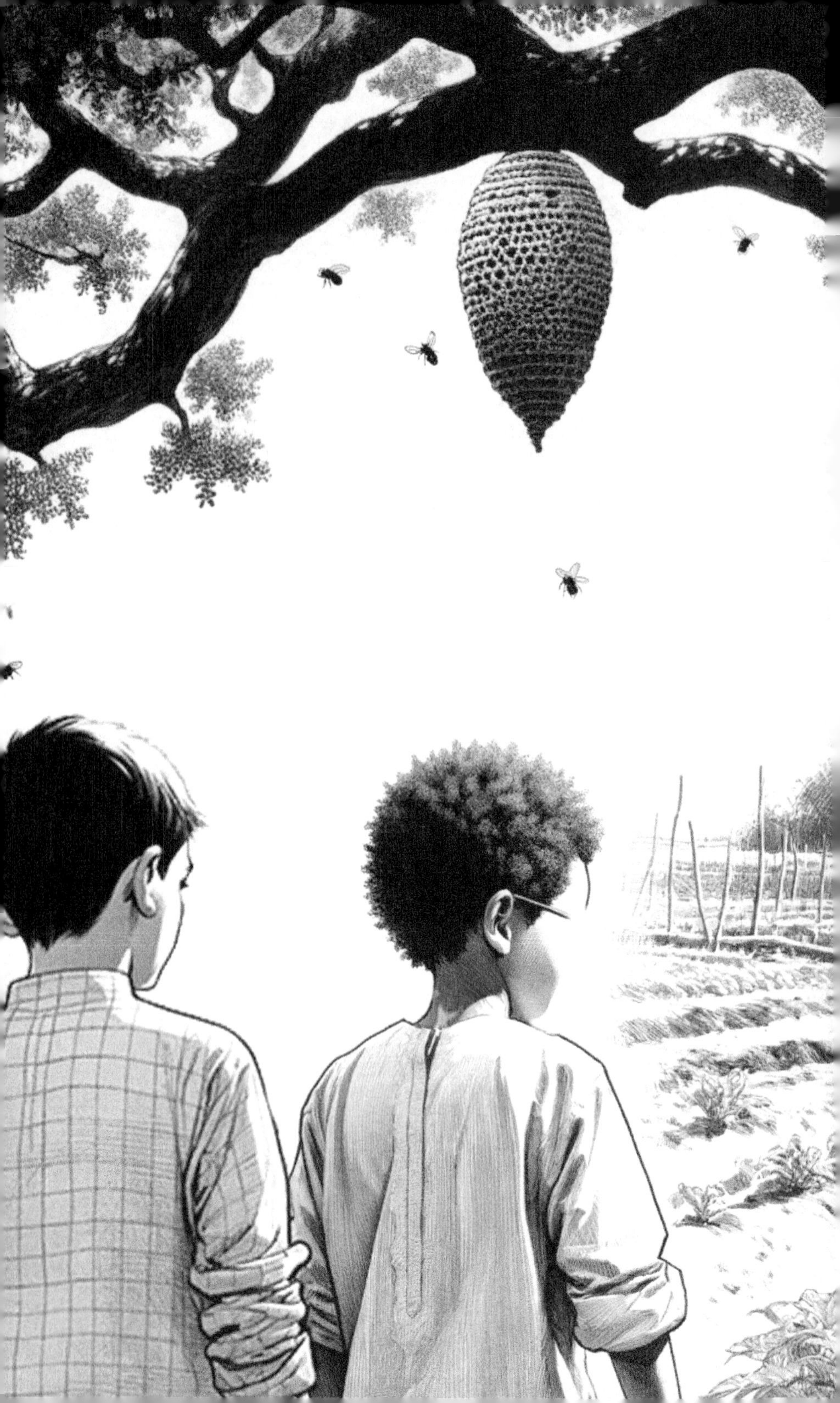

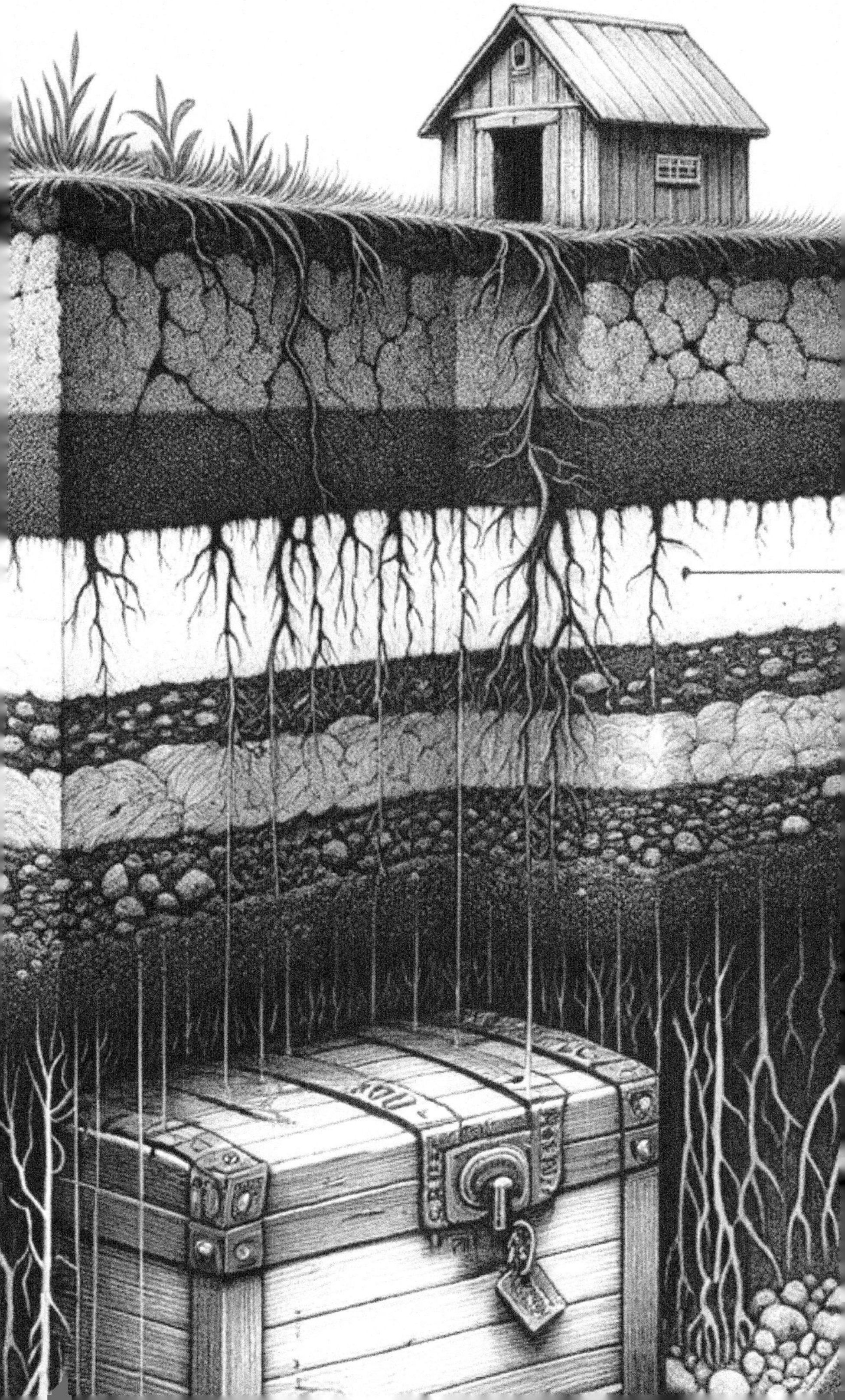

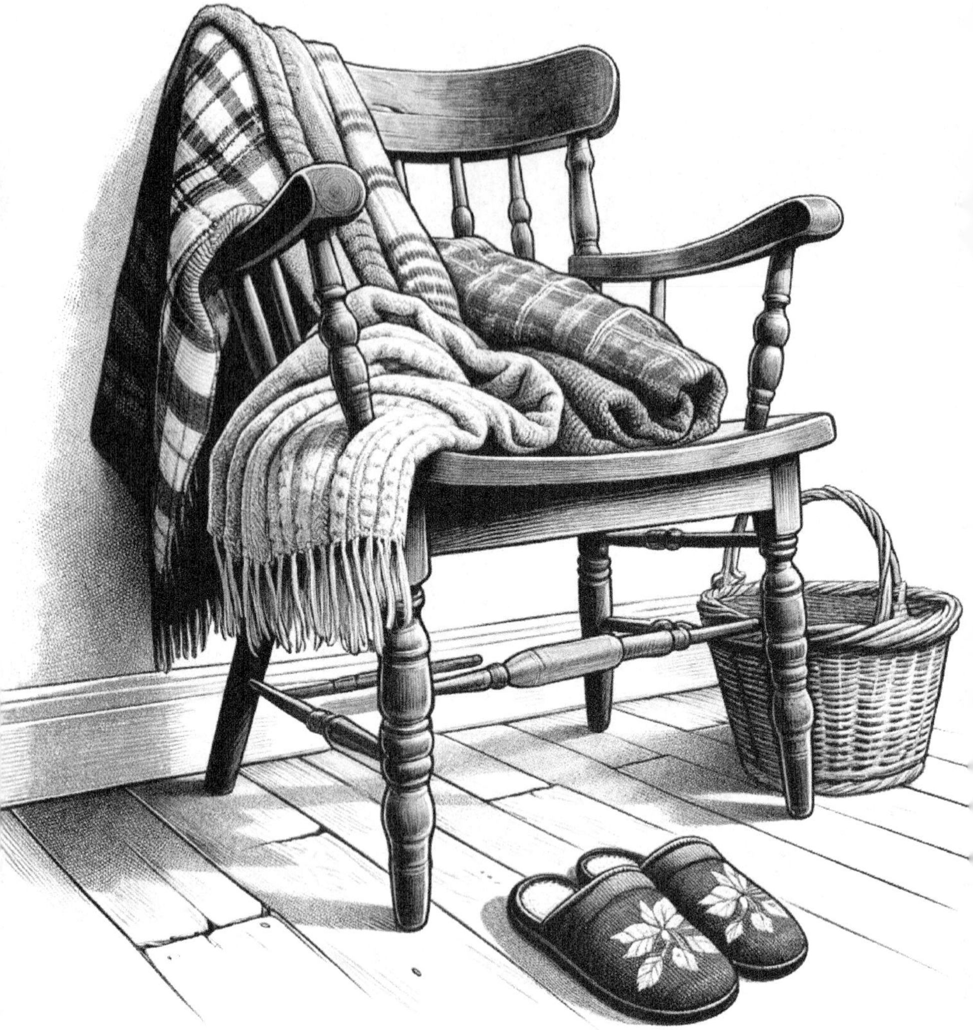

Chapter 13:
A Legacy of Love

On a sunlit Friday afternoon, Abdullah joined his father and grandfather on a trip to the local Masjid for the Jumuah prayer. Every Friday, Abdullah devotedly performed Ghusl, used perfume, and cleaned his teeth with Siwak.

Moments before leaving, Ummi, with a loving smile, leaned down and whispered to Abdullah, "Abdullah, remember, sunscreen is your skin's shield from the sun's sneaky rays, just like a brave knight's armour. Keep safe, and go conquer your day!"

The Three Hakeems set off downtown, enjoying the warm sunlight, and melodious chirps of birds. Abbi, with a mischievous glint in his eye, attempted to bond with his son. "The last one to the top of the hill is the king of the barn for a week!" he dared Abdullah.

Abdullah's face lit up with a bright smile. The cheerful Abbi he knew was back. "You're on, Abbi!" he declared.

With laughter echoing in the air, they raced to the top of the nearby hill, joy in every step. Abbi reached the highpoint first, and they all burst into laughter.

"Don't worry," Abbi encouraged Abdullah, "The more you try, the better you get. Plus, you're destined to be a top-notch farmer, young man, insha'Allah," he teased his son, referring to his barn-cleaning forfeit.

"Ha ha. Hilarious," Abdullah responded, with sarcasm.

Grandpa Luqman chuckled softly as he watched his son and his grandson playfully joke on the hills. Their laughter was a joyful sight that brought warmth to his heart, reminding him of life's continuing beauty amidst sorrow which gently eased the pain of his hidden grief.

Moments before entering the Masjid, Abdullah gazed at Abbi, "We're a team, aren't we?"

Abbi chuckled warmly, "Absolutely, Habibi."

Abdullah's eyes sought reassurance, "And you'll always be there for me, won't you?"

Abbi's expression softened, understanding his son's need for connection. His gaze drifted skyward, Abdullah followed his gaze. "Listen, Abdullah," he started, "whenever you seek guidance, remember, *Allah (The Most High) says, 'Call upon me, I will respond.'*"

Abdullah nodded. They both admired the moment, feeling a strong connection, knowing guidance was always just a Dua away, to Allah (The Most High).

While father and son engaged in their playful activities and precious moments, Grandpa Luqman busied himself with the Dua for entering the Masjid. He whispered the words under his breath and felt the weight of his years. The Dua held a special place in his heart, a reminder that Allah (The Most High) guided him in all he did.

Abdullah, with his curious nature, noticed his grandfather's quiet devotion, his youthful heart eager to share in the sacred moment. Just as he decided to follow him, Grandpa Luqman finished reciting the Dua, and turned to Abdullah, quoting,

"The Prophet Muhammad (peace and blessings be upon him) said, 'When one of you enters the Masjid, let him send salutations upon the Prophet then say: O Allah! Open for me the gates of Your mercy. Then, when he exits, say, O Allah! I ask You of Your bounty.'"

Abbi caught up, with grandpa leading. The three Hakeems walked together, quietly supplicating to their Lord. Three generations connected by faith, walked towards the Masjid, finding solace in the powerful Dua.

As they entered the busy Masjid, the soothing echoes of the Iqamah filled the air. They made their way to the front row, where an elder man, even older than Grandpa Luqman, was preparing to lead the prayer, his voice strikingly familiar to Grandpa Luqman.

Abdullah's eyes scanned the familiar faces. Everyone was cheerful and content, looking their best, with the scent of perfume in the air. The room was a mixture of boys and men from diverse backgrounds. Feeling a deep sense of belonging, Abdullah's heart swelled with joy, knowing he was part of a larger family united by their love for Allah (The Most High), and The Prophet Muhammad (peace and blessings be upon him).

As the congregation gathered for Jumuah, they listened to the Khutbah before concluding with the Friday prayer. The Khateeb's words carried a heart-warming message about the fleeting nature of life. He urged everyone to cherish each day as if it were their last, for none knew when their time would come. He repeated the words from the Quran *"every soul shall taste death."* The words echoed in Grandpa Luqman's heart as he embraced the familiar voice. Abdullah sat quietly near his father and grandfather, taking in every word, and reflecting on life's purpose.

The words inspired Abdullah to reflect on his future and what he wanted to achieve in life. He remembered Grandma Jamila, her legacy of kindness, and boundless love that continued to shape their family. He realised that his grandmother had left a deep impact on him, one that continued even after her passing. Determined to follow in her footsteps, Abdullah was filled with newfound purpose.

As they left the Masjid, the golden sun continued to shine, warming their path home. Abdullah's heart swelled with hope and determination. He understood that becoming truly wise, like his grandfather, and loving like his grandmother, was a lifelong journey, and he was ready to embrace it.

The three Hakeems quietly left the Masjid, reciting the Dua for exiting. As they walked on their way home, they approached the same hill they ran up earlier, and Abdullah couldn't help but share a playful idea. "Abbi, you know, instead of racing down the hill, how about we race backwards? It would be fun and funny!"

Abbi and Grandpa Luqman shared amused glances and agreed. They made their way to the hill, running backwards with fits of laughter, making an already sunny day even brighter. It was moments like these that brought them closer as a family, reinforcing their bonds and filling their hearts with joy.

Looking back on how Abdullah had grown from being scared and resistant to accepting the changes in his life and enjoying companionship, he realised that true resilience came from embracing growth and learning from others he can trust. He believed that his family's legacy of faith, love and wisdom would guide him on this journey, just as it had for generations before him.

Chapter 14: Sweet Memories

Along the way home from the Masjid, Grandpa Luqman's keen eyes caught sight of an old neighbour, Mr. Shareef, whom he hadn't seen in a while.

"My brother Luqman, it's been ages!" Mr. Shareef exclaimed, his eyes lighting up as he chuckled.

"Grandpa, that's the Imam from the Masjid today!" Abdullah exclaimed, displaying his observational skills.

Grandpa Luqman's eyes lit up, realising the familiar voice at the Masjid was his old neighbour's. They greeted warmly then Mr. Shareef's eyes softened as he said, "I heard about your wife. She was such a lovely lady, always so kind and caring."

Grandpa Luqman nodded, "Indeed she was. May Allah (The Most High) have Mercy on her and Forgive her."

Mr. Shareef spoke softly, his words carrying a heartfelt Dua, *"May Allah magnify your reward, and make perfect your bereavement, and forgive her."*

For a brief moment, they reflected on Grandma Jamila's kindness and the times she had shared her delicious recipes with their neighbours. Their conversation wandered through memories of her.

Mr. Shareef smiled fondly as he shared his recollections. "I remember her fascination with honey. She had quite the collection of honey jars, didn't she?"

Grandpa Luqman chuckled, his eyes crinkling at the corners. "Oh, yes. She dreamed of selling honey from our own bees one day. She believed it would bring joy and a cure to others, insha'Allah."

Mr. Shareef nodded in agreement. "Such a sweet dream, just like her. She had a heart of gold."

As Abdullah and Abbi followed behind Grandpa Luqman, Abdullah couldn't help but overhear his grandfather's conversation with Mr. Shareef about Grandma Jamila's love for honey. This conversation sparked his interest and desire to do something special in her memory.

Mr. Shareef continued, "You know, Luqman, it's not quite like back home in Palestine, is it?"

Grandpa Luqman's heart skipped a beat. The mention of Grandma Jamila's homeland, a place known for its exceptional honey, triggered a deep longing within him.

He looked at Mr. Shareef with a thoughtful expression. "You're right," Grandpa Luqman admitted. "Well, I've been thinking lately, perhaps it's time for a journey of my own. Back to Ethiopia, where I come from. Both Palestine and Ethiopia have a rich history of producing some of the finest honey in the world."

Mr. Shareef nodded in understanding. "A journey to your roots, Luqman. Sounds like a wonderful idea." Their conversation stirred feelings in Grandpa Luqman, knowing that the memory of Grandma Jamila and her dreams had the ability to inspire new beginnings.

Spotting Abdullah, Mr. Shareef asked about him. "He's a strong young man," Grandpa Luqman said proudly.

Abdullah approached and greeted Mr. Shareef, his respect shone through. "As-Salaam-Alaikum, Sir. My grandpa always says that everyone we meet can teach us something. What advice can you give me?"

Mr. Shareef's smile widened as he offered his advice, *"Be kind, yet cautious with your trust, and always judge fairly. And stand firm for your religion because Allah (The Most High) says, 'neither will you fear nor grieve.'"*

Abdullah humbly replied, "A great reminder, Sir."

Mr. Shareef, impressed by Abdullah's manners, asked Abbi if he'd ever thought about travelling abroad with Abdullah to seek knowledge from the scholars. He suggested Abdullah could inspire the city's youth. The idea of Abdullah travelling left Abbi deep in thought.

Before Mr. Shareef bid farewell and continued on his way, he rummaged through his pocket, presenting Abdullah with a gift, "Here, take this book of Ad'iya. It will be like a companion for you when you need guidance. Oh, and a bottle of perfume for you."

"Grandpa, look!" Abdullah exclaimed. "I always wanted a book of Ad'iya for memorising. And I love perfume. Jazakom Allahu Khair, Sir. This means a lot to me."

The three Hakeems felt the warmth of their interaction with the kindly elderly neighbour.

A silent thought deepened in Grandpa Luqman's mind as they continued to walk home. Then, he spoke with a newfound intention, "You know, I've been thinking, I need to make Hijrah to a Muslim country while I still can, insha'Allah. It's something we've always hoped for," revealing his shared dream with Grandma Jamila.

The weight of his words hung in the air, and Abdullah and Abbi exchanged empathetic looks, knowing the importance of Grandpa Luqman's decision. They all walked home in reflective silence.

As the three Hakeems returned home mid-afternoon, they noticed their new neighbour, Tony, with another boy his age, outside, Jake. Abdullah gathered his courage and whispered to Abbi, "Can I introduce myself to the newcomers? You know, kindness to neighbours."

Abbi nodded and continued towards home with Grandpa Luqman. Tony turned to see Abdullah walking towards him as Abdullah asked politely, "Hey, have you, um, seen anything odd around our place today? We were out, and we have some animals in the farm."

Tony shook his head, but his friend, Jake, surprisingly, blurted out, "Actually, there was a man askin' for you. He said his name was Frederick Lupas or somethin'."

"You mean Patrick Lucas." Tony corrected. The name sent a shiver down Abdullah's spine. A sudden tension filled the air, and Tony sensed his discomfort.

"Yeah, that guy," Jake replied quickly, his gaze suspicious as he looked Abdullah up and down. "So, what's with the bees, man? Don't you have any real friends?" he added, laughing mockingly.

"I don't get it," Abdullah replied, confused. In his home, respect came naturally, so he never imagined meeting someone so unkind. For the first time, he faced bullying. As Tony and his friend continued to laugh, Abdullah's determination to uncover the truth about his farm and the recent neighbourhood events only grew stronger, without anybody trying to stop him.

With Tony and his friend's laughter still echoing in his mind, Abdullah carried the weight of the moment back into the safety of his home. The disrespect he encountered was a complete contrast to the values upheld within these walls, where respect and kindness were instilled into their daily lives. Conflicted yet fuelled by a resolve to seek answers and make a difference, Abdullah found solace in his home.

Snapping out of his thoughts, Abdullah heard his mother call out from the back garden, "Abdullah, can you come here, please? There's something we want to show you." Her voice, carrying a blend of secrecy and excitement, diverted his attention from his unsettling thoughts.

Stepping into the backyard, Abdullah was met with a heart-warming sight that would redefine his understanding of family support and the collective pursuit of passions. Ummi and Ramlah stood beside a beautifully assembled honeybee project of their own, their faces lit with anticipation and joy.

"We've been working on this together," Ummi began, gesturing towards the charming setup nestled safely away from the garden's play areas. The project was a big pot of vibrant collections of bee-friendly flowers, sugar water feeders, and cosy shelters designed to attract and nurture more bees, especially with cooler weather on the horizon.

"It's amazing!" Abdullah exclaimed, his eyes scanning over the thoughtful details of the project. "But why?"

Ramlah, bouncing excitedly, was quick to answer. "Because we love the bees too! And I found a different spot to play with my ball, so I won't bother them."

Ummi's gaze softened as she added, "And, Abdullah, we've missed Grandma Jamila a lot. She would have been so proud of your dedication to the bees. This ornament for the bees is our way of honouring her legacy, together as a family."

The surprise humbled Abdullah, washing away any traces of doubt about his family's understanding of his passions and their collective grief for Grandma Jamila. The bee ornament wasn't just a gift; it was a legacy.

"Jazakom Allahu khair. Grandma would've loved this. It's like, um, a bee cafe!" he exclaimed.

As they spent the rest of the afternoon discussing plans to expand the café and brainstorming ways to further educate the community about the importance of bees, Abdullah felt a profound sense of belonging and purpose. The bullying incident, though still fresh in his mind, seemed less daunting now, overshadowed by the love and support surrounding him.

That evening, as they gathered in the cosy living room, Abdullah looked around at his family—Ummi, Abbi, Ramlah, and even Grandpa Luqman, who had joined in to admire the day's work—and realised that together, they were unbreakable. The bee café had not only brought them closer but had also increased Abdullah's determination to protect the bees and spread awareness about their crucial role in the ecosystem.

In that moment, Abdullah knew that no matter what challenges lay ahead, he had the best team by his side. And with a renewed sense of hope and a heart full of love, he whispered a silent prayer of gratitude, feeling more connected to his family and to Grandma Jamila's memory than ever before.

Chapter 15: Whispers in the Dark

The night before Abdullah's big presentation was filled with restlessness. Abdullah had been preparing for weeks, carefully researching and creating a captivating presentation about bees from the Quran. He felt confident until the weight of his recent worries began to occupy his thoughts.

In the dimly lit room, Abdullah sat at his desk, hunched over his presentation poster. His mind was racing with thoughts—his beloved grandmother's recent passing, his grandfather's decision to make Hijrah, the secret about the keepsake box, the unsolved mystery about the beehive and burglary, the approaching end of his summer Islamic studies class, and the sudden realisation that he'd be sharing a room with his little sister, Ramlah, during the presentation night. The stress was almost too much to bear, and the clock on his wall ticked away harshly.

As Ummi tucked Ramlah into bed before hurrying down to the kitchen, Abbi was downstairs reciting the Quran in the living room. Meanwhile, Grandpa Luqman got ready for bed upstairs.

Unexpectedly, the home phone rang, breaking the evening silence. "Abdullah, could you answer that, please?" Ummi's voice floated from the kitchen.

Abdullah ran downstairs and answered, pressing the phone to his ear, waiting silently for the caller to speak. "Assalamu Alaikum, Merhaba, it's Yusuf."

With relief on his face, Abdullah exclaimed, "Wa Alaikum Salam, Merhaba, bro! So glad it's you!"

"How's it going?" Yusuf inquired. "How's your project for the presentation coming along? Made any headway with the beehive thief?"

Abdullah took a deep breath in, leaning against the wall. "There's still a lot to do on my project. And about the beehive thief... I'm sure there's something out there, but Abbi's forbidden me from digging deeper. I want to respect his commands, you know?"

Yusuf's voice softened, "Yeah. I'm sorry. That's tough." He shifted the topic, trying to lighten the mood. "Well, I completed my project on spiders. My father actually let me handle spiders and tarantulas for it. Super cool stuff," he bragged.

"Wow, that's cool! Your father sounds cool. May Allah (The Most High) bless him. Why can't my father be cool like yours?" Abdullah half-joked, half-serious.

Humbled, Yusuf replied, "Everyone's different, you know." Just then, Abbi walked by, overhearing Abdullah's words. A pang of hurt hit him, but he remained silent, choosing to keep walking.

Unaware of his father's presence, Abdullah confided, "It's just... I want Abbi to see I'm trying. It's tough at home, especially since grandma passed. I just want him to support me, to trust me more, and my goals."

Yusuf, sensing his friend's pain, offered his empathy, "Bro, listen. I know it's hard but remember your blessings. And maybe try talking to your father? He might be a better listener than you think."

"Yeah. Maybe you're right," Abdullah admitted. "I just want him to be proud of me," he added. "Thanks."

Yusuf said, "Always."

"How about hanging out at my place tomorrow after lesson?" Abdullah suggested.

"Count me in!" Yusuf agreed enthusiastically.

Abbi, now at a distance, reflected on Abdullah's words, realising that he needed to be more supportive and a better listener to his son's passions and worries. It was a moment of self-reflection, a silent promise to bridge the gap he hadn't noticed forming.

The call ended, but Abdullah's words hung in the air, a reminder to Abbi of the role he played in his son's life— not just as a protector but as a supporter of his goals.

While saying goodnight to his parents, still unaware that Abbi overheard his call, Abdullah ascended to his room. He passed his old room, noticing Grandpa Luqman reciting the Quran, then settled at his desk, gazing at his unfinished poster for another half an hour.

Abdullah took a deep breath, uncertain about his ability to deliver the presentation he had diligently been preparing for. Just as his confidence faded, a gentle knock interrupted his thoughts. It was Grandpa Luqman, a comforting presence in his moment of need. He entered the room, with a smile on his face, looking at his grandson. As the door gently swayed open, Abdullah was greeted by the delightful smell of freshly baked Kanafeh, which filled the air with its mouth-watering scent. Downstairs, Ummi had been preparing the traditional pastry late into the night.

It was specifically for Abdullah's eventful day tomorrow; a special day, marking the end of Abdullah's summer Islamic studies class, and each student was expected to bring their favourite dish from their respective countries. Ummi wanted to ensure a special treat for the occasion.

As Grandpa Luqman fixed his gaze on Abdullah, he whispered softly, "Late-night preparations, my boy?"

Abdullah nodded gently, grateful for his grandfather's presence and support. "It feels incomplete, Grandpa."

Grandpa Luqman continued, "Remember, there's no time like the present. And while I prefer the Quran and authentic Ahadith to any other quote, here's a saying that may inspire you: 'Don't watch the clock, do what it does. Keep going.' You've put in the effort, my boy, and I believe you'll deliver your best, insha'Allah."

Abdullah smiled, then looked down at his presentation. "You know, Grandpa. It's just... well, everything feels too much right now."

Grandpa Luqman sat down beside him, his voice gentle as he spoke. "Abdullah, Allah (The Most High) tests us in different ways. But these tests make us stronger. Just as a bee faces obstacles in its quest for nectar, you too can overcome your obstacles and deliver your message with confidence, insha'Allah."

Abdullah poured his heart out to his grandfather, his voice trembling with sadness. "It's just— Sometimes, it feels like everyone I care about ends up leaving. First grandma, then the bees. Who's next? You? Tomorrow's my last lesson, and I might not see my friends again. We might not even go camping. What should I do?"

With the wisdom of his years, Grandpa Luqman gently replied, "That's a lot on your young shoulders, but my boy, life is a journey filled with comings and goings. People are like travellers; they enter and exit our lives like passengers on a train. Those who leave often make room for new companions to board. Cherish the moments you have with those you love, for each interaction may be your last. In your solitude, find strength; in your strength, find faith; and in your faith, never give up. Remember, trust Allah's plan (The Most High). Tests prepare us for great rewards yet to come."

Abdullah looked both inspired and a bit puzzled by the depth of his grandfather's words. "Whoa, Grandpa, that's a lot to remember!" Abdullah chuckled.

Grandpa Luqman smiled and summarised his wisdom in one profound sentence: "Listen, my boy, remember this – *Life's comings and goings shape us for the journey ahead.* Trust Allah. Just like bees collect nectar to make honey, sometimes the most unexpected things can lead us to answers we've been searching for."

Suddenly, Abdullah's eyes sparkled with realisation. "That's it, Grandpa! Just as Grandma mentioned!"
Grandpa Luqman, puzzled, asked, "Mentioned what?"
Abdullah exclaimed, "The trail!"
Grandpa Luqman, leaned in. "Who has a tail?"
Abdullah chuckled. "No, Grandpa, it's about the bees."
"Bees have a tail?" Grandpa Luqman wondered aloud.
"No!" Abdullah laughed, trying not to disturb Ramlah's sleep, "Grandma left clues about the beehive thief. She knew who it was and wanted us to uncover it."
Grandpa Luqman's face lit up with understanding. "Ohh. So, what's the plan now, my boy?" he whispered.
Abdullah said with determination, "The plan is to trust Allah's plan. I've got this insha'Allah."

Grandpa Luqman stood to leave, advising, "Do what you must, my boy. Just make sure you stay safe."

Abdullah nodded, grateful for his grandfather's support, and asked if he knew a Dua for confidence. Grandpa Luqman reminded him of Mr. Shareef's gift.

"My Dua book! Jazakom Allahu Khair, Grandpa," Abdullah beamed, searching for his book.

As Grandpa Luqman left, Abdullah felt achievement and reassurance. He continued working on his presentation with renewed intentions, adding the finishing touches to his poster.

The night wore on and Abdullah noticed his little sister sleeping soundly on her side of the room. He couldn't help but smile at her innocence, even though her presence might make it harder to concentrate.

After deciding to get some much-needed rest, a familiar sound echoed through the room—a late-night cat show. Miza had chosen the most inconvenient time to seek Abdullah's attention and serenade him with her 'cat recital.' He tried to gently shush Miza, but she seemed determined to continue. Abdullah's patience was tested as Miza's loud meowing filled the room.

As he lay in bed glancing at the ticking clock, it was well past midnight. He was torn between sleep and Miza's serenade, he couldn't help but think the night held more challenges than he had imagined, and all his negative thoughts returned to him, leaving him in a state of uncertainty about what tomorrow's presentation would bring. He closed his eyes, whispering a heartfelt Dua to Allah (The Most High), knowing that despite life's worries, he wasn't alone.

Chapter 16: Unexpected Turns

Saturday morning filled Abdullah with excitement and hope as he readied himself for his final weekend Islamic studies class. Unlike most children who might grumble about weekend school, Abdullah couldn't wait for today. He had a special opportunity to share two things close to his heart – the incredible world of bees and a piece of his heritage.

Abdullah, dressed in his favourite white thobe, rushed out, bumping into Abbi, who playfully remarked, "Whoa, slow down! Did a bee sting you?" Abbi chuckled.

"Sorry, Abbi," Abdullah replied, excitement in his voice. "Today's my presentation day, and I woke up this morning feeling ready. I think I'm ready, Abbi. Please, make Dua to Allah (The Most High) for my success."

Abbi replied, eager to show his support, remembering Abdullah's phone conversation last night, "May Allah (The Most High) grant you success, Habibi. You'll do fine. Just stay focused. Now travel safely. I'll see you at dinner, insha'Allah." Abdullah smiled, appreciating his father's kind words and heartfelt goodbye.

Ramlah suddenly popped up, blurting out, "Bodi, your skin is like bee wings, with pretty marks!" referring to his vitiligo, her eyes glowed with innocence.

Abdullah chuckled, ruffled her hair, and said, "Thanks, Beady Eyes, you're absolutely right! Bazzzzz!" he playfully poked Ramlah like a buzzing bee.

Abdullah was about to head out again when Ummi gently halted him, reminding him to take a special dish for after his class presentation, Kanafeh, knowing it was his favourite dessert.

"Oh, thanks, Ummi!" Abdullah exclaimed with a big smile on his face. "I knew I smelled Kanafeh last night!"

Ummi chuckled warmly and replied, "Enjoy your day, my dear son, and don't forget your sunscreen." She then embraced Abdullah, planting a tender kiss on his forehead and bidding him farewell, "Assalamu Alaikum, my dear. Now go conquer your day."

Abdullah left home with his mother's love, favourite treat, father's Dua, sister's jests, grandfather's wisdom, best friend's support, and most importantly, his trust in Allah (The Most High). He was fully prepared to share his presentation with his classmates.

With a big grin on Abdullah's face, he headed off to his lesson, smiling all the way. As he approached his class with enthusiasm, he found his classmates huddled around the classroom door. A note pinned to the door announced from their teacher, Mr. Hameed, "Sorry, lesson's cancelled today. Postponed for next weekend."

A shadow of disappointment crossed Abdullah's face; he had stayed up late preparing. Minutes later, Yusuf arrived, and upon hearing the news from Abdullah, they decided to head to Abdullah's place early.

"Let's go, c'mon," Yusuf suggested, eyeing the dish in Abdullah's hand. "Is that Kanafeh you've got?"

"Yeah. It's a Palestinian specialty," Abdullah replied, a hint of pride in his voice.

"Nice! My mum makes that too!" Yusuf exclaimed, excited by the similarity. "But today, I brought Baqlava, a Turkish dessert."

"Cool! Baqlava is popular in Palestine and Ethiopia too," Abdullah noted, appreciating the diverse selection.

As they walked towards Abdullah's home, the conversation shifted from desserts to more personal matters. Yusuf noticed Abdullah's usually bright mood had dimmed slightly since the morning's change of plan. It's as if all his troubles returned suddenly.

"Hey, you've been kinda quiet. Everything okay?" Yusuf asked, his voice laced with concern.

Abdullah breathed in deeply, feeling a mix of frustration and sadness. "It's just... ever since my grandma passed away, it's been tough. And with today's presentation cancelled, it just reminds me of how I have no control over what happens next."

Yusuf nodded, empathising with his friend. "I'm sorry about your grandma, bro. Losing someone is never easy. But you know, talking about it, especially with your family, can help a lot. And remember, it's Allah (The Most High) who is in control of everything."

"Yeah, I know," Abdullah hesitated before continuing. "I know I'm being tested. It's just... Since my father forbade me from searching for the beehive thief, I feel like there's something missing. He won't listen to me."

Yusuf halted Abdullah, "Your dad cares about you, Abdullah. Maybe he's worried it could be dangerous. And you know, obeying parents in good is important. They usually have reasons for what they say."

Abdullah pondered over Yusuf's words, the conflict within him evident. "I guess you're right. I just need him to see things from my perspective too."

"Maybe he does, more than you realise," Yusuf offered with a gentle smile. "Like I said before, why don't you talk to him? Share how you're feeling, not just about the thief but about missing your grandma too. I'm sure he misses her just as much. I mean... you always talk about working together as a team, right? Well, maybe this is your chance to prove it."

The idea seemed to offer Abdullah a new perspective, one that made him question his determination to stand for what he believed in, and if he truly respected his father's requests. "I didn't think of it that way. Jazak Allahu khair, Yusuf. I'll try talking to him tonight insha'Allah. May Allah (The Most High) make it easy."

"Ameen! And remember, I'm here for you, okay?" Yusuf reassured Abdullah, trying to put his mind at rest, "Anytime you need to talk or even just to hang out."

As they neared Abdullah's home, the conversation lightened, discussing hobbies, friends, and plans for the presentation. Abdullah carried with him a renewed sense of understanding and a plan to bridge the gap between him and his father. His mood shifted from disappointment to hope, realising that even in moments of loss, there's always a way forward.

Suddenly, their light-hearted conversation came to an unexpected halt when Tony and Jake stepped out from around the corner, blocking their path with a smirk.

"What's this? Food for the homeless?" Jake mocked, eyeing the Kanafeh in Abdullah's hand with disrespect.

Before Abdullah could react, Jake reached out, purposely knocking the box of Kanafeh to the ground, the contents spilling onto the path. "Oops," he taunted, "why don't you do somethin' about it, weirdo?"

Tony, who had been trailing behind Jake, laughed at first, finding amusement in his friend's cruel behaviour. However, as the situation escalated and Jake refused to back down, Tony's laughter faded. "C'mon, man, let's go. He's not worth it," he muttered, a hint of reluctance in his voice.

Yusuf, anger flaring at the injustice, stepped forward, his loyalty to Abdullah steadfast. "Hey, what's your problem? Your parents never taught you manners?" he challenged, his voice steady despite the rage simmering beneath.

Jake and Tony exchanged looks, their laughter echoing off the buildings as they mocked Abdullah and Yusuf for being "different" and "weird." Their cowardly retreat left Abdullah in a state of shock, the joy of the day's earlier conversation overshadowed by the harsh reality of bullying.

Yusuf, still boiling with anger, turned to Abdullah. "Are you okay?" he asked, his concern evident.

Abdullah, trying to mask his hurt, nodded. "Yeah, I'm fine. Thanks for standing up for me," he said, his voice barely above a whisper.

Together, they continued to Abdullah's home, the ruined Kanafeh was a silent proof to the cruelty they had faced. As they approached the door, Abdullah's heart weighed heavy with the decision to downplay the incident. He couldn't bear to add to his family's worries.

The day's lessons were harsh but valuable. Abdullah understood that the journey ahead would require bravery—not just in facing bullies but in opening up to those who cared about him most.

Upon returning home unexpectedly early, Abdullah's family was surprised. After explaining the day's change of plans, they gathered for an early lunch. Abdullah couldn't help but notice a serious look on his father's face, but decided to wait and see if he was okay.

Confusion crossed Ummi's face as she opened the bag with the Kanafeh. She immediately noticed the damaged dessert. "What happened to the Kanafeh?" Ummi inquired, her jaw dropped in shock.

"It's no big deal. I accidentally dropped it," Abdullah lied, forcing a smile to reassure his mother.

His parents exchanged concerned looks but chose not to press further, sensing Abdullah's discomfort. The room was filled with silence and unspoken questions, and the morning's joy replaced by a quiet tension.

Feeling the awkwardness, Yusuf signalled Abdullah to speak up after his meal. Seizing the moment, Abdullah asked, "So, are we still on for camping after my presentation?" reminding his parents of their yearly awaited event.

Ummi smiled, "What a fun idea!"

Abbi hesitated, worry in his eyes. "Sorry, Habibi, we can't manage a camping trip right now."

Abdullah's smile faded. "That's okay, Abbi. Maybe we'll camp outside, you know, in the garden?"

Suddenly, Abbi stood, looking troubled. "I'm sorry, excuse me," he muttered, leaving the room. Ummi glanced at Abbi with concern and followed him, leaving Abdullah and Yusuf pondering in the room, confused.

Abdullah noticed their heated discussion in the kitchen about an unexpected bill. A £500 heating oil expense posed a financial challenge for their low-income family.

Unable to ignore the tension any longer, Abdullah decided to break the silence, hesitating, he asked with concern in his voice, "Did I say something wrong?"

A heavy atmosphere filled the room as Abbi prepared to share some news. Using a gentle tone, he hoped to ease the effect. "You said nothing wrong. It's just— I'm sorry but we can't continue home-schooling you."

The room fell silent as everyone absorbed the news in their own way. Abbi and Ummi shared a look of mutual understanding. Grandpa Luqman sat composed, his steady gaze offering stability. Ramlah, oblivious, looked for comfort in her parents' faces, fidgeted with her doll. Abdullah felt a rush of emotions.

"I should go," Yusuf said, swiftly exiting with a promise to catch up later.

"Bro!" Abdullah pleaded his friend. Then quickly turning to Abbi, "Abbi, is this my fault?" Abdullah's voice shook.

Abbi quickly reassured him, "No, Habibi, this isn't about you. I need to provide for this household. Supporting Grandpa Luqman's Hijrah is important to us, yet it means making some sacrifices as a family. Ummi and I need to work full-time while you attend school in the city. This change is temporary, insha'Allah."

"A city school?!" Abdullah exclaimed, disappointed.

"Bodi, what's the city like?" Ramlah asked.

"Busy, I guess." Abdullah mumbled, suppressing his thoughts and emotions again.

Abdullah cherished his home-schooling, a time filled with learning and shared moments with his family. But now, it seemed that this chapter was coming to an end. His heart ached with the thought of leaving behind the comfortable life he had grown to love.

His parents exchanged sympathetic looks. It was a tough decision, but they were prepared to make sacrifices for the family's well-being wherever possible and determined to face any challenges.

Abbi responded gently, "Abdullah, this decision wasn't easy, and it's not meant to hurt you. We believe it's for the best, considering our family's needs and future. Remember, we're doing this together, and we're here to support you through this transition. Your happiness and well-being are our top priorities."

Sitting with a worried expression, Abdullah looked down as he silently took in the news. Deep inside, his patient nature was already thinking of ways to make the most of this change, "I get it, Abbi. Change happens. Home-schooling is great, but you know what, I'm ready for new adventures, insha'Allah."

"Darling, I see you're trying to be strong for us. But, we're here to listen," Ummi reassured gently. Just then, her words triggered weeks of Abdullah's hidden grief and unspoken fears, and his feelings rushed to the surface, causing him to lose his temper.

"Listen?!" Abdullah yelled, feeling ignored. "Nobody here listens. Decisions are made, paths are chosen, but what about what I want? It's like I don't even matter."

The room fell into silence, all eyes on Abdullah. Ummi, understanding Abdullah's need to feel heard, said firmly, "Abdullah, we've all been trying to listen. Maybe not perfectly, but differently. And remember, it's Allah (The Most High) who truly Hears and Sees all."

Abbi, who had sensed this moment coming, recognised the importance of a breakthrough, and approached his son. "Abdullah, lower your wings of mercy," he advised. "It's true. We've been so focused in our ways that we've missed your side. I'm sorry. But we need action now."

Grandpa Luqman, with wisdom, added his perspective gently. He understood the need for this decision. "Abdullah, my boy, life is full of surprises. I've seen many in my time. Like bees find their way to flowers in new fields, we too must learn to adapt and find beauty in changes." Relief spread as his voice filled the room.

"Thanks, Grandpa," Abdullah murmured, his eyes misty. Ramlah, sensing her brother's distress, wrapped her arms around him. "Thanks, Ramz," he sighed.

Grandpa Luqman smiled, hoping to lighten the mood. "See, we thrive on unity as much as on solitude." He then shared a prophetic saying to comfort Abdullah. *"The Prophet Muhammad (peace and blessings be upon him) said, 'How wonderful is the affair of the believer, for his affairs are all good, and this applies to no one but the believer. If something good happens to him, he is thankful for it and that is good for him. If something bad happens to him, he bears it with patience and that is good for him.'"*

Abdullah felt a mix of emotions — understood yet overwhelmed. Realising his perspective wasn't the only one, his heart sank further as he processed the effects of this decision. The comfortable life he knew was slipping away. Without hesitation, he turned to his parents and asked, "So, what will you do for work?"

Abbi, unable to hold his excitement any longer, replied, "Well, about our jobs, we've decided to do beekeeping together, following your grandparents' path. We're ready. So, planning to start tomorrow, insha'Allah."

Abdullah's jaw dropped. "Beekeeping?!" he exclaimed. "As in, working with bees? But I love bees! I could work with you too," he suggested, with a glimmer of hope.

"We can't, Habibi. This is a job suitable for adults. It's not safe for children. But your support means everything," Abbi gently explained.

In that moment of realisation, Abdullah felt defeated and remembered his place. "Yeah, for adults. Safety first." Abdullah said quietly, aiming to keep his tone respectful. "I, um, need some time alone. I'm sorry I raised my voice." He forced a smile, masking his pain.

Climbing the stairs, he realised they no longer creaked, and guilt flowed through him. He regretted speaking harshly to his parents, recognising they were only trying their best. A deep longing for the comfort of his home already began to cave in on him, and he couldn't bring himself to accept his reality.

The familiar routine they had come to love was changing, and they would need to adapt to a new reality, one that involved school schedules, text books, new faces, and new places.

Chapter 17:
Shopping with Ummi

With the new school year fast approaching and the summer coming to an end, Abdullah and Ummi went on a shopping adventure to gather the necessary supplies.

Ummi tried her best to make it an enjoyable outing, but Abdullah's hesitance cast a shadow over their trip.

They strolled through the aisles of the department store, searching for school uniforms, textbooks, and stationery. Ummi chattered away, pointing out colourful backpacks and shiny new lunchboxes, but Abdullah's responses were short, and his gaze drifted aimlessly.

While browsing the store, Ummi noticed Abdullah's gaze lingering on a plush bee nestled among teddy bears. Leaning towards Ummi, Abdullah whispered, "Can we get this bee teddy for Ramlah? I'll miss her when school starts."

Seeing the rare spark of fascination in his eyes amidst their shopping, Ummi felt a twinge of guilt. She could sense Abdullah missed his old routine.

Quickly picking up the last few items on their list, Ummi tried to win her son over with a sweet treat. "How about some ice cream after this?" She suggested a visit to a local ice cream shop with Yusuf and his mother. This idea brought a faint smile to Abdullah's face.

Basket in hand, they moved towards the checkout, Abdullah's thoughts still with the bee teddy.

Suddenly, a loud voice startled Abdullah in the shop. "Arrgh! I never get what I want!" the voice echoed.

Abdullah grinned but then noticed Tony behind him in the queue, fussing to his mother about school preparations. Catching Abdullah's grin, Tony shot back a stern look, causing Abdullah's grin to fade and leaving him with an uneasy feeling. It was clear that Tony was challenging.

Tony's mother, used to her son's outbursts, replied, "You can't always get what you want, when you want."

Eager to start a conversation, Ummi noticed the matching uniforms, and asked Tony's mother, "Is your son going to West City High School too? The all-boys school?" Their options for nearby schools were limited. West City, located in the city, impressed Ummi for its excellent grades, praised conduct, and good reputation.

Tony's mother nodded politely. "Yes, he'll be starting there soon. It's just like any other school, I suppose." Tony rolled his eyes, mimicking his mother, "You know, boys will be boys." She added. He had heard her say this many times before which she believed meant that some behaviours were just typical for boys.

Ummi nodded, though she wasn't entirely sure what Tony's mother meant by *"boys will be boys."* She made a mental note to ask Abbi about its meaning later.

Abdullah, sensing Tony's negativity, knew effort to connect was needed since they were going to attend the same school. Eager to bridge the gap between them, he extended his right hand for a friendly handshake. "Hi. I didn't introduce myself properly before. I'm Abdullah. Nice to meet you."

Tony looked at Abdullah's hand, then mumbled, "Uh, sorry, I don't do handshakes," avoiding eye contact. His mother nudged him, feeling embarrassed by his rudeness. In that moment, Abdullah felt a wave of rejection he had never experienced before. After another nudge, Tony reluctantly accepted, "Okay, fine." He shook Abdullah's hand, leaned in, and whispered, "Stay out of my way, okay?" his tone threatening.

The two mothers continued their chit-chat, sharing tips for preparing to go to school. During the conversation, Tony's mother revealed her recent separation from her husband, and their plan to move to the city. As they said their goodbyes, Ummi was left with a sense of uneasiness about the upcoming school year.

Down at the ice cream shop, Abdullah and Ummi joined Yusuf and his mother for a treat as promised.

"Sorry you couldn't figure out where the trail leads," Yusuf said, breaking into Abdullah's thoughts.

Abdullah smiled regretfully. "I wouldn't dare go into my neighbour's meadow, but I can't help thinking there might be more beehives there or something."

Their mothers exchanged glances, overhearing their excitement. "You boys and your wild adventures," Abdullah's mum chuckled.

Yusuf's eyes sparkled with mischief. "Imagine the honey those hives could hold! Pure gold, bro!"

"Yeah," Abdullah agreed, his mind racing with ideas. "Maybe there's a way to find out without trespassing." Catching Ummi's warning look, he chuckled, and quickly added, "Or maybe not. I give up anyway."

They continued chatting away quietly, the thrill of the unknown bonding them further, their mothers shared a knowing look, amused and slightly concerned by their sons' endless curiosity.

As they peacefully enjoyed their ice creams, Abdullah's gaze darted to the window, spotting Mr. Lucas passing by. A sudden rush of adrenaline flowed through Abdullah's veins, and he felt a strong urge to follow him.

"Go on, bro!" Yusuf encouraged. "We'll watch your things and finish our ice creams insha'Allah." Grateful for his best friend's support, Abdullah swiftly pursued Mr. Lucas, Ummi followed, calling Abbi on her phone.

When Abdullah caught up with Mr. Lucas, he couldn't hold back the question that had been bothering him all summer. "Mr. Lucas," Abdullah's voice trembled with determination, "d-did you take honeycombs from my beehives?" His heart pounded in his chest.

Mr. Lucas turned to Abdullah, his tone tinged with annoyance. "Oh, look, it's the bee whisperer kid. What are ya gonna do about it? Sting me?"

Mr. Lucas tried to ignore Abdullah, but he persisted, "Mr. Lucas, stealing is wrong!" he exclaimed, "Those honeycombs were a gift from my dead grandma!"

Mr. Lucas halted and turned towards Abdullah, feeling shame, "Listen, I—" he sighed. "I took the honey for my wife. She's ill. I know it's wrong but I was desperate."

Empathy began to fill Abdullah's heart for Mr. Lucas. He knew the pain of loss and how desperation can lead to mistakes, much like his own experiences. He wanted to understand his reasons and offer a chance to fix it.

Chapter 18: The Queen's Fate

During their exchange, Abdullah noticed several bees flying near Mr. Lucas. "Mr. Lucas, are you wearing something sweet?" he asked, recalling how certain scents attract worker bees.

"No. Why?" Mr. Lucas replied with a puzzled look.

Approaching slowly, Abdullah saw Mr. Lucas holding a jar with a queen bee inside, "Mr. Lucas, where did you get that queen bee from?" he asked, tilting his head.

Overwhelmed by fear as bees swarmed around him, Mr. Lucas waved his hands, trying to shoo them away, while a small crowd gathered, watching in shock. "Help!" he cried out, panicked.

In this crucial moment, Abdullah faced his greatest challenge yet: to aid the man who had wronged him. He stepped closer, urging, "D-don't move! I can help you."

Upon arriving at the scene, Abbi reassured Mr. Lucas with confidence in his son, "He knows what he's doing. Let's give him a moment. You got this, Abdullah."

Abdullah began, "Bismillah. They're after their queen in your jar. They're following her scent. They won't hurt us if we're calm," his knowledge shining through.

Abbi helped manage the crowd, ensuring their safety, "Please, everyone, step back a bit and give us some space. We don't want to alarm the bees."

Mr. Lucas, realising he had wronged the only ones trying to help him, was overcome by guilt. "Enough," he confessed quickly, "I can't hear well. I stole the queen bee and honeycombs. Just get 'em off me, quick!"

Everyone felt a mix of emotions as Mr. Lucas finally confessed. In a brief moment, the crowd went quiet, shocked. Abdullah was surprised and hurt, while Yusuf and his mom looked at each other, not really surprised. Abbi seemed disappointed yet a glimmer of respect for the honesty finally shown. Ummi gasped, feeling sorry for Mr. Lucas. But despite the stealing, they all still wanted to help him.

Watching her son and husband manage the situation, Ummi silently supplicated to Allah (The Most High), placing her deep trust in Him to guide them through. With a heart full of faith and eyes fixed on the unfolding scene, she witnessed Abdullah's courage as he slowly moved in to take the jar, now swarmed by buzzing bees. As Abdullah reunited with his queen bee, he declared, "We need to get her back to her hive before the cold sets in."

He began to carefully guide them away from Mr. Lucas and the crowd, observing his surroundings for a safe place. Then, ensuring the queen bee was secure in the jar, still covered in a swarm of bees, Abdullah took decisive action. With Mr. Lucas still swatting at bees, Abdullah, Ummi, and Abbi moved quickly. Ummi, noticing several manmade beehives in the back of their open-bed truck—a new addition for their beekeeping business—joined them.

As they prepared to depart, Ummi climbed into the truck's cab with Abdullah and the bee-covered jar, while Abbi assisted a nervous Mr. Lucas into the front seat.

Yusuf handed over their shopping bags then dashed back to his mother, who stood a safe distance away, waving them off. "You got this, bro!" he shouted, offering support. The crowd burst into excited discussion as the family drove off safely towards home.

Throughout the drive, Abdullah nervously yet determinedly held the jar, focusing on the bees' humming vibrations. Ummi, ever supportive, reminded him, "You're doing amazing, Abdullah." Her words boosted his confidence, making him feel as though he was indeed destined for this role.

Mr. Lucas, now calmer and grateful for Abdullah's brave act, expressed his gratitude, "Hey kid, what you did was crazy and heroic, especially for your age. Thanks." The tension between them transformed into mutual respect.

Abbi, proud of his son, remarked, "You're handling this like a true beekeeper. May Allah keep you steadfast!"

Mr. Lucas offered a sincere apology from the passenger seat. Abbi, concentrating on the road yet mindful of the forthcoming discussion, said, "Hold that apology for now; we have a nation to raise," hinting a deeper conversation later.

Arriving home, Grandpa Luqman and Ramlah, previously unaware of the day's events, were quickly greeted and reassured by Ummi about everyone's safety. With Abbi's close supervision every step of the way, Abdullah carefully proceeded to place the queen bee back into her hive.

And then, Grandpa Luqman halted them, causing alert. "Wait, my boy! Unity matters, but only on the correct path," he declared, drawing everyone's attention.

"Grandpa?" Abdullah was taken aback by his sudden presence. Grandpa Luqman warned them of the dangers, "Take it slow. If we rush and don't do it right, the bees may not accept her back, or worse, they could hurt her. We need to make sure we return the queen home but safely. Patience is key." He advised.

His last words echoed in Abdullah's head. "Patience is key." Abdullah mused aloud. In that moment, the knowledge he gained during the summer, came to light. "Grandpa, would you like to take over?" he offered, understanding what this would mean to him.

Grandpa Luqman nodded, accepting the challenge. It was the first time, since Grandma Jamila's passing, that he was going to handle the bees. Abdullah slowly took a step back, shaking the bees off his hands, as Ummi and Ramlah observed anxiously through the window.

Grandpa Luqman took the lead, his every move watched closely. He began by placing the jar near the hive entrance, allowing the bees inside to calm down and adapt to their surroundings. "It's all about patience and trust," he murmured, his focus steady.

Next, he slightly opened the jar to let the hive's scent mingle with the queen's, an important step to ensure the bees inside would recognise her as their leader. As Abbi sprayed the bee smoker towards the bees, the tension increased; would the bees accept her, or not.

After a few tense moments, Grandpa Luqman carefully removed the lid entirely, but he didn't rush to release the queen. Instead, he waited, letting the bees inside the jar and those in the hive interact at their own pace. "The queen's pheromones are key," he explained. "They need time to spread and be accepted."

Finally, with the jar open and the queen exposed, the hive's workers tentatively approached the jar, their antennae twitching, testing the air. The family held their breath, hoping for a sign of acceptance. "Did they accept, Grandpa?" Abdullah asked, losing patience.

Then, as if a silent agreement had been reached, the workers began to fan their wings, a behaviour used to spread the queen's scent throughout the hive— a clear sign of acceptance. Relief washed over everyone as Grandpa Luqman smiled, "She's their queen, no doubt."

"Allahu Akbar!" everyone exclaimed, with Mr. Lucas joining in. "Allah Akbar," he echoed, not fully grasping its meaning. Everyone smiled at his innocent attempt.

Grandpa Luqman's skill turned a dangerous situation into a lesson about harmony and understanding, showing how nature needs careful handling and deep knowledge to live with it.

The remaining bees from the jar slowly gathered into the hive, joining the colony in an unbroken transition. And it didn't end there. While observing the bees closely, Abdullah noticed them collecting nectar from a trail of flowers leading from the nearby meadow to the hive, and more bees joined, drawn to the queen. Suddenly, it clicked. Grandma Jamila's other note about following the trail where flowers bloom finally made perfect sense. It was a beautiful moment witnessed by everyone, with profound lessons for all.

Thousands of bees, each with their unique role, buzzed within the hive. This was more than just saving a queen bee; it was a lesson about the importance of different roles, the value of teamwork, and how trusting Allah (The Most High) can lead to answers we search for.

This experience marked a pivotal moment in Abdullah's journey, illustrating his growth in courage, compassion, and his ability to unify a community, not just the bees but his own family and neighbourhood.

As the atmosphere lightened, Abbi insisted on a private talk with Mr. Lucas, Abdullah stood nearby. Meanwhile, Grandpa Luqman returned indoors, preparing to pray.

"I'm sorry," Mr. Lucas began, revealing his financial struggles and his wife's illness, for which he believed honey to be a cure. Hesitant to impose on the Hakeems following Grandma Jamila's death, he saw no other choice at the time. He denied any involvement in the burglary, clarifying that it was a setup by a jealous neighbour who discovered his honey-stealing. He wanted to apologise to Abbi for taking honey without asking but couldn't find him. Every failed attempt only tempted him to steal. Today, upon seeing Abbi's active bee smoker by the tree, he acted on impulse, using it to calm the bees before taking the queen bee.

Observing his sincerity, Abdullah explained, "Grandma wanted to help and left clues in her notes. The bees living in our tree have been collecting nectar from Mr. Lucas's old meadow to make honey in our tree, which he has been seeking. Grandma wanted me to learn this: to use our honey to help those in need." After returning Mr. Lucas's hearing aid, Abdullah sought his father's permission, "Can we help him with the honey, please? It feels like the right thing to do. It's what Grandma would have wanted."

Abbi agreed decisively on the condition that Mr. Lucas stops stealing, highlighting the value of honesty and community support. Mr. Lucas, gratefully accepted, "Mr. Hakeem, ya kid would make a superb beekeeper."

Chapter 19:
New Supplies, New Hope

Late afternoon, Abdullah returned home with his father, carrying the bags, from the truck, filled with newly purchased school supplies. Their shopping trip had been tiring, with Grandpa Luqman taking an extra nap upstairs, but Abdullah's success in solving the mystery of the missing honeycombs made it all worthwhile.

"Abdullah, I'm sorry for doubting you about Mr. Lucas," Abbi said, showing regret. "Forgive me?" he pleaded.

Abdullah, feeling a great sense of accomplishment, responded with a hint of humour, "Thanks for believing in me, Abbi! If you ever need a detective for your business, just call me, 'The Bee Whisperer Master.'"

A grin widened Abbi's face as he enveloped his son in a heartfelt hug. "I'm so proud of you!" he declared.

Ramlah eagerly shuffled through the shopping bags. Her eyes sparkled with curiosity as she explored each item. However, it was the plush bee that immediately captured her attention. With a giggle, she grabbed the soft toy and dashed to her room, her imagination taking flight as she began a playful conversation with her new fuzzy friend, "Hello, Bazzy! Let's have a tea party!"

Abdullah glanced at his mother and couldn't help but smile. Ummi's thoughtful gesture had not gone unnoticed, and he appreciated the small attempt to make the transition to school a bit more bearable. As Abdullah's eyes fixed to the ground, the room fell silent.

Abbi, sensing Abdullah's worry, gently prodded him, "Habibi, I know this change is hard. Talk to me."

At the peak of his emotions, Abdullah opened up. "It's just... I know the decision's been made, but I'm gonna really miss home-school," he admitted, feeling a surprising warmth as tears rolled down his cheeks.

For the first time, Abdullah fully expressed his feelings. He shared his sadness over losing Grandma Jamila. He spoke about his hesitation to leave his last Islamic studies lesson, his friends, and his hobbies behind. It was a pivotal moment in his emotional journey.

His parents enveloped him in understanding and support. They reassured him, with similar feelings. "You know what? I'll miss it too—home-schooling you," his father admitted. "And I miss your grandma, my mother."

Ummi added, "It's been hard for me too. I've missed Grandma every day, and now, I'm going to miss having you near, daily. But we are in this together."

This shared moment deepened their bond, helping Abdullah to feel validated. It emphasised the value of family support and open communication.

In the comforting warmth of his parent's embrace, Abdullah found the courage to voice a concern that had weighed heavily on his heart. "There's something else," he hesitated, the words catching in his throat. "At the shops today... We saw Tony and he, um, will be going to the same school as me. I didn't realise this before. But... but Tony and his friend have been bullying me. I just have a bad feeling about them, you know."

Abbi's eyes widened. "Tony? The neighbour's boy?"

"Yes!" Abdullah explained, "He says stuff that hurt." Abdullah detailed the incidents, his voice changed, speaking of Tony's harshness and mocking laughter.

Abbi sat down, disappointed in himself for failing to be there for his son in his time of need. "I'm sorry I wasn't there for you, Habibi. I had no idea. I promise to do better insha'Allah. And you know, in the real world, not everybody wants to be your friend. Some people will already make up their minds about you before even giving a chance to get to know you. They just don't feel good about themselves," he explained gently, his face mirroring Abdullah's sadness. "Listen, give him a chance, though. Everyone has a turning point. And if this continues, I'll speak with his parents insha'Allah."

Ummi, trying to recollect the day's events, nodded in agreement, her hand reassuringly on Abdullah's back. "It's true. Facing this will make you stronger, and remember, all the prophets went through similar tests, and worse. You know, maybe Tony is going through a difficult time too. Perhaps he needs a friend like you."

Empowered by his parents' advice and understanding, Abdullah nodded, a newfound resolve in his eyes. He decided then that he would try to talk to Tony, to understand him, and perhaps, find a way to bridge the gap between them.

Just then, the doorbell rang, slicing through the evening calm. Abbi answered the door to find Tony's mother standing by the entrance, her expression apologetic.

"Mr. Hakeem, I just came by to say I'm so sorry about my son's behaviour towards yours earlier," she began, her apology sincere and genuine. "Tony," she called over her shoulder, "come here, please."

As Tony stepped forward, he looked less threatening than Abdullah remembered, "I'm sorry, man," he said, his eyes rolling to the side, "I was wrong."

Abdullah, although surprised, accepted Tony's apology, nodding. "It's okay. Maybe we can start over?"

Tony's mother smiled, grateful for Abdullah's generosity of spirit. "Thank you," she whispered before they left.

Closing the door, Abbi turned to Abdullah, a proud smile spreading across his face. "I knew you could do it," he said, his pride in his son evident. "You handled that with more maturity than many adults would."

As they settled back into the warmth of their living room, Abdullah felt a lightness he hadn't known in weeks. The day's events had taught him about the power of forgiveness, the strength found in facing one's fears, and the unbreakable support of family.

Abbi took a deep breath, "Abdullah, I've been thinking to allow you a small role in our beekeeping business."

"Really?!" Abdullah burst out, "I've learned lots about beekeeping, Abbi. It's my passion. I promise to be responsible and follow your guidance, insha'Allah."

Abbi nodded, "Provided it doesn't interfere with school."

"You're the best father I could ever ask for," Abdullah said, finally realising his father's silent support all along.

Entering the room, Grandpa Luqman gave Abdullah a gentle nudge. "You know, you're quick to adapt," he observed, "like your bees," he added. They both laughed, knowing it wasn't the end of their strong bond.

As laughter replaced their tears, Ummi and Abbi settled side by side on the sofa, their voices hushed. Ummi, with a curious look, turned to Abbi and inquired, "What exactly does 'boys will be boys' mean?"

Abbi paused for a moment, considering his words carefully. He looked at Abdullah, who was sitting at the nearby table, and replied, "Well, 'boys will be boys' is an old saying, but it's not an excuse for bad behaviour. It means that sometimes, boys tend to be adventurous, energetic, and maybe a bit naughty as they grow up. However, it doesn't mean we should overlook their actions or let them get away with anything. It's our responsibility as parents to guide them and teach them the correct way, so they grow into responsible and respectful young men."

Abdullah couldn't quite hear their conversation but noticed the serious expressions on their faces. He turned his attention back to Grandpa Luqman, feeling reassured by his father's wise words. Curious as ever, he asked his grandfather if he ever attended a school when he was younger.

"Ah, Abdullah," Grandpa Luqman began, his eyes twinkling with memories, "When I was young, schools were few, often miles away from where we lived. Most of us couldn't dream of attending them. Instead, we learned through community gatherings, where elders shared their wisdom. I also spent many nights reading by the flicker of a lantern, teaching myself from any book I could find. And, of course, much of my youth was spent working on the farm, learning the hard work that comes with tending to the fields. Those were our classrooms, Abdullah, under the open sky."

"You were home-schooled too!" Abdullah exclaimed.

Grandpa Luqman felt a wave of nostalgia as he shared his distant memory. "Schools come in many forms, my boy. My mother was my first school. Life experiences are often a better teacher than a classroom. But school shouldn't limit your goals. It's all about how you use it."

Abdullah leaned back deep in thought, realising that perhaps the changes since his grandmother's passing were all a distraction from his grief, reminding him that life, like a clock, always moves forwards. He reflected that it's not about what happens to us but rather how we respond, knowing that one day we'll meet our Lord, Allah (The Most High), and be questioned for all we did.

As a gentle patter of rain trickled down the windows, Ummi and Abbi rushed to shelter the animals into the barn. The season began to change, and Autumn was near, bringing with it cooler temperatures.

A smile brightened Abdullah's face as he moved to lean towards the living room window, gazing at the perfectly intact beehive outside. He observed fewer bees outside. Inside the hive, they grouped together for warmth, minimised the entrance, and focused on indoor tasks like caring for young and managing food stores, ensuring their survival through the cooler, wet weather.

As the evening drew in, the family gathered before dinner in the cosy living room, by the warmth of the crackling fire, each holding a Quran. Together, they recited, taking turns, uniting in faith and mentally preparing for the challenges of the approaching year.

Miza circled Abdullah's legs, purring as she settled at his feet. He playfully greeted her, "Hey there, MizMiz! Where have you been hiding? Are you gonna miss me too?" He stroked her while continuing his recitation.

Chapter 20: Abdullah's Big Day

As summer began to transition into autumn, school was quickly approaching, and the rescheduled day for Abdullah's presentation and last Islamic class had finally arrived.

This Saturday mirrored the previous one, with Abdullah awakening to a similar rush of energy, though this time tinged with a hint of nervousness.

Dressed in his favourite white thobe, Abdullah added a dash of perfume after completing his morning routine. The air buzzed with excitement as he darted through the hallway, colliding with Abbi, who teased, "Careful there! You're as eager as a bee heading to its hive!"

"Oops, sorry, Abbi," Abdullah replied, barely containing his eagerness. "It's presentation day, and I'm just feeling a bit nervous. Please keep me in your Ad'iya."

Abbi, his smile beaming with pride, offered a sincere Dua, "May Allah (The Most High) make your path easy today, Habibi. You're braver than you think, and your energy is contagious! We'll be waiting to hear all about it tonight, insha'Allah."

Chiming in, Ramlah, with her usual innocence, complimented, "Bodi, you're strong as beeswax!"

"Thank you, Beady Eyes," Abdullah responded, playing along with her imagination. "I'll bring back some sweet treats for you later insha'Allah!"

On his way out, Ummi stopped him with a reminder, her hands presenting the Kanafeh lovingly prepared for his class. "Your favourite, to celebrate after your presentation," she said, her eyes gleaming with love.

Gratefully taking the dish, Abdullah exclaimed, "It's going to be a great day, Ummi, insha'Allah!"

With a final, warm embrace from Ummi and a cheerful "Assalamu Alaikum" sending him off, Abdullah stepped outside, once more, armed with the love and support of his family, the excitement for his presentation burning brightly within him.

While Abdullah cherished his moments with family, he also valued the companionship of his like-minded friends from his Islamic studies class. In their multicultural class, he greeted Yusuf showcasing his language skills, "Assalamu Alaikum, Merhaba, Yusuf!"

Yusuf grinned back and replied, "Wa Alaikum Salam Wa Rahmatullahi Wa Barakatu, Abdullah! Merhaba! Are you ready to inspire the class today?"

The two had been friends for as long as they could remember. Their friendship had grown over the years. Abdullah's mixed ethnic background and Yusuf's Turkish heritage made their bond unique. Together, they shared a passion for exploring different cultures while embracing their Muslim identity. Their classroom was also a blend of city and farm boys.

Observing others as they confidently presented their works, Abdullah quietly recited the Dua he memorised from his Dua book, *"O my Lord! Open for me my chest, ease my task for me, and make loose the knot from my tongue, that they understand my speech."*

Student after student showcased their projects, sharing their ideas and knowledge. Posters were hung up on the walls of their small-sized classroom. Soon, it was Abdullah's moment to step into the spotlight and unveil his findings to his classmates.

The classroom buzzed with anticipation as students gathered, and Abdullah couldn't have been more prepared. His presentation was not just a product of research. It was based upon his own interests, upbringing, and legacy of his late grandmother. His family had instilled in him an appreciation for bees and honey, particularly from Palestine and Ethiopia.

Standing nervously before his classmates, Abdullah hesitated, clearing his throat. "Ahem—I, um, err..." After a moment of tension and awkward silence, he slowly began his presentation, "Assalamu Alaikum. Bismillah." He looked around the classroom, then continued, "Today, I, um, want to talk to you about something truly inspiring – the world of bees. You see, bees are more than just insects; they're amazing creatures that play an important role in our lives. They're like nature's superheroes, and they've amazed me since I was little."

As Abdullah presented his research on bees, he displayed a poster showcasing his findings. He started by reciting the Quran from Surah Al-Nahl (Chapter of The Bee), specifically verses 68-69, emphasising how Allah (The Most High) honours bees in the Quran.

With enthusiasm, he explained that these verses held valuable lessons about the importance of bees and their hard work, how even the smallest creatures in the natural world could serve as signs from Allah (The Most High). His classmates listened carefully, captivated by the wisdom Abdullah shared.

For a brief moment, Abdullah thought about his late Grandma Jamila. "Now, as some of you already know, my grandmother recently returned to Allah (The Most High). She was very knowledgeable about bees. She taught me that bees teach us that every life matters."

He added, "I have a mixed background. I'm British, and my family is from Palestine and Ethiopia, where some of the best honey in the world is made. These countries have a long history of beekeeping, and the honey is really famous because of its unique quality and taste."

Abdullah's peers listened carefully, interested in his personal connection to honey and love for his heritage. He felt a profound sense of pride in sharing his knowledge and it humbled him.

Continuing with confidence, Abdullah shared stories of real beekeeping practices back home, emphasising the importance of bees in agriculture and the environment, "I want to talk about Palestinian honey – a treasure from the land that's close to my heart. Palestine, with its rich history and diverse flora, offers unique varieties of honey like wildflower, citrus, and thyme, each with its distinct taste and healing properties." The room filled with curiosity as Abdullah spoke of the challenges and resilience of Palestinian beekeepers, and how honey signifies success and wellness in Palestinian culture.

With a light-hearted touch, he joked, "I think bees mistake me for a flower because of my perfume scent and spots," referring to his vitiligo, bringing smiles to his classmates' faces.

He concluded, "Bees teach us that every role matters. If a wise leader and a hard-working community come together, like them, I believe we can change the world."

Slowly but surely, his confidence grew as he observed his classmates' expressions change from curiosity to wonder. The more he spoke, the more they became genuinely interested in bees, honey and beekeeping.

Abdullah persevered, "Bees are so good at adapting to change, so why can't we? And like, how bees help their hive, do we help our homes the same? Also, they're super loyal to their queen, what's that teach us about teamwork? Why can't we be like a bee community?" He thanked his classmates politely then returned to his seat, saying, "Jazakom Allahu Khair for listening!"

Abdullah's presentation sparked engaging discussions, with his words noticeably influencing classmates' views on animals and diverse cultures.

Suddenly, a single voice whispered, "Bee whisperer." This quickly spread as others joined in, creating an echo of admiration. Before he knew it, the whole class was energetically chanting "Bee Whisperer! Bee whisperer! Bee whisperer!"

Despite his visible shyness, Abdullah couldn't help but feel a sense of pride. His unique connection with nature had touched the hearts of his classmates, and his words had reached them. The idea of teaching others began to take root in his mind. As he reflected, his grandfather's voice echoed, *'Life's comings and goings shape you for the journey ahead.'* Those words felt like a golden stamp of inspiration in Abdullah's heart.

Mr. Hameed, his teacher, had to calm down the excited class and praised Abdullah for his hard work. He raised his hands, signalling for silence. "Settle down, everyone," he chuckled. "May Allah (The Most High) bless Abdullah for his dedication and hard work."

After class, everyone gathered for a special lunch to celebrate the end of the summer Islamic studies season. It was a pleasant feast, filled with laughter and cultural discoveries.

Bilal, another classmate, from India, brought a dish spiced with turmeric and ginger, explaining, "In India, honey and bees are important too. My mum says India could have millions of bee houses aiding the farms." He couldn't help but add, "And you know what? In India, these spices, just like bees, are small but mighty, and also have healing properties."

Abdullah, fascinated, responded, "Wow, Bilal, that's so cool! I didn't know bees and spices were such a big deal in India. Your dish sounds cool too with all those spices. May Allah (The Most High) bless it."

Approaching Abdullah, Yusuf exclaimed, "Bro! Your presentation was super cool! You stood firm and opened our eyes to bees, honey, and culture. I'm proud to have a friend like you. Your grandma would've been so proud of you. May Allah have mercy upon her!"

Abdullah felt a rush of emotions, realising that moments like these were not only just about sharing knowledge but also about uniting a diverse background upon good. From that day forwards, Abdullah was known as the 'Bee Whisperer' in his community.

The excitement of Abdullah's successful presentation lingered as he returned home that afternoon with Yusuf. His family gathered for a celebratory meal of 'Maqluba,' his favourite dish. Bursting with joy, Abdullah shared how great his presentation went. As he shared the details, he noticed Abbi's eyes light up with pride. "O Habibi, we knew you'd do great!" Abbi affirmed.

Bonus Chapter: The Gift of Wisdom

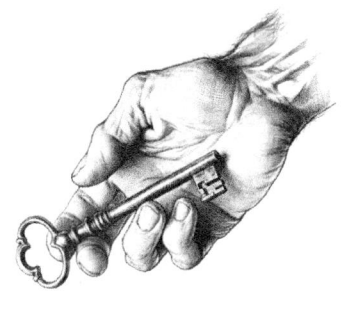

Over the next few days, Abdullah swayed between nervousness and excitement following the family's recent decision about his schooling.

Upstairs, Grandpa Luqman took his usual afternoon nap, undisturbed by the household's quiet movements. In the living room, Ramlah was lost in an adventure with her bee teddy, while Ummi managed the beekeeping business's finances in her office corner.

It was then that Abbi, dressed in his beekeeping suit, saw the opportunity to fulfil his overdue week-long promise to his son. With a father's love guiding him, he approached, calling out, "Ya Habibi!" Noticing Abdullah's downcast gaze, Abbi with concern, approached. "Everything okay?" he asked.

Abdullah's reply was simple yet profound. "Abbi, how will I travel to a city school from our farm?"

Abbi, holding his thoughts with understanding, began, "Remember Mr. Shareef?"

"Yes, Abbi. What about Mr. Shareef?" Abdullah responded, his curiosity mixed with confusion.

Abbi explained, "Well, he suggested Uncle Musa continue his security job at a nearby library, nightshift. Your uncle accepted and offered to drop you to school and back every day." He added, "And it turns out, Umar, your cousin, will be attending the same school."

Abdullah bit his lip, "Tony and Umar at the same school as me? Subhan Allah!" he said, his voice tinged with surprise. "Well, that'll be an interesting experience."

As a meaningful reminder, Abbi recited, *"Perhaps you dislike a thing which is good for you"*. He added, "Habibi, trust your instincts, but trust Allah even more."

"You're right, Abbi," Abdullah replied, apologetically.

And so, with a heartfelt tone, Abbi moved in to fulfil his promise. He opened his hands to reveal a well-kept family treasure—a small, antique key passed down through the generations. It was the key to the keepsake box buried in the garden; the final piece to the puzzle.

Abdullah looked up to see his father, captivated by his beekeeping suit as he handed him the old yet shimmering key, and asked, "What's this key for, Abbi?"

Abbi replied, "This, Habibi, is a key to our family's most treasured gift. It's time you learned what's inside that keepsake box."

The mystery of the hidden keepsake box was now just a key turn away, and a final note that read:

"A dream with no action is like no sun but a moon."

Suddenly, as if a fog had lifted, Abdullah's eyes widened with excitement and curiosity. "What's in it, Abbi? Why was it a secret for so long?"

Abbi smiled, feeling a mix of nostalgia and relief. "Habibi, you are one tough character you know that? Always looking for answers," he remarked, his tone full of pride, "that's what makes you special."

Abbi continued, "You see, it was all about emotional healing, respecting everyone's process, honouring your grandma's requests, and bringing you a nice surprise. Your grandparents, especially Grandma Jamila, wanted this to be a special surprise for you when the time was right. Inside that box is a gift—a gift that will connect you to the wisdom and love they shared with us. Allah (The Most High) tests us all the time. Trusting His plan and Qadr is important; it brings peace, knowing our tests are from His wisdom for the best outcome."

In the quiet corners of their hearts, Abbi and Abdullah held a profound understanding of the reasons behind their secret-keeping. They knew that, above all, it was about Grandpa Luqman's emotional healing. By allowing him to grieve at his own pace, they hoped he would find solace and strength. It was about honouring the wisdom of their elders. Moreover, it was about trust, patience, helping those in need, and following a legacy.

They believed that by respecting Grandma Jamila's requests for Grandpa Luqman's happiness and wellbeing, they were honouring her in a beautiful way. And the surprise, like a hidden treasure waiting to be discovered, was intended to bring a heart-warming joy into the Hakeem family's lives when they needed it most. Their strengthening bond was proof that Grandma Jamila had a deep understanding of her family when she planned this gift.

Abdullah, feeling both nervous and excited, said, "This feels like a big responsibility, Abbi."

Abbi chuckled, his gaze turning to the shimmering key. "Let me tell you this, Abdullah: inside that box holds the key to our family's history, a legacy of love, and an inheritance that will guide you in the journey of life."

Abdullah reflected on his father's words, his excitement now fuelling his hope. "I can't wait, Abbi. I can't wait to understand it fully when I open it insha'Allah."

Grandpa Luqman, who was silently listening, surprised everyone with his wakefulness as he suddenly spoke. "That's not just any old key, my boy. It is a symbol of the strong bond between generations. Your journey with it will be a test of your faith, your character, and your commitment to carrying forwards the legacy of those before you, which we derived from the Quran and Sunnah, with the understanding of the Salaf."

Abdullah nodded, feeling a deep sense of responsibility and determination. "I'm ready, Grandpa. I'll make sure to honour this legacy, insha'Allah."

With the key now unveiled, it became a source of inspiration and motivation for Abdullah, a reminder of the wisdom and love that would guide him on his path.

Abdullah's heart fluttered with zeal. The evening held a promise of treasures yet to unlock. As he stood beside his grandfather, a newfound sense of unity enveloped their family. The decision to bring Grandpa Luqman into their home had solidified their bonds, but tonight, they would dig deeper, both metaphorically and literally.

Abdullah turned to his wise Grandpa Luqman and asked, "O Grandpa, would you mind showing me how to dig again, just for old time's sake?"

Grandpa Luqman always said that knowing how to dig was a beneficial skill. "Digging," he'd say with a smile, "is a skill that brings us closer to the earth, and the earth holds secrets we can't understand until we seek them." Tonight, that wisdom would become clear.

Abbi joined them, spade in hand, as Abdullah stood around the mysterious burial site. "Are you ready, Abdullah?" Abbi asked, his tone eager and determined.

Abdullah nodded and took the spade from Abbi's open hands. "Bismillah. Let's do this together."

They dug in unison, the soil moving to their shared determination. The soft thud of earth against metal echoed in the night as the moon shone from above. Abdullah's heart raced with every shovelful of soil, closer to the keepsake box that held his grandmother's memories and treasure.

Finally, the edge of the box emerged from the earth like a shimmer of hope. Abdullah gently cleared the soil away, revealing the worn but still sturdy wooden box. The old brass key hung from the palm of his hands, entrusted to him by Abbi, passed down through generations, and now his responsibility.

Abdullah gazed at the keepsake box, feeling a wave of nostalgia rush over him. He recalled a distant memory of a time when his beloved Grandpa Luqman showed him a similar box when he was just a little boy.

As Abdullah slowly turned the key and lifted the lid, a bunch of sealed envelopes greeted his eyes. Each one had a packet of flower seeds attached to the back. Alongside, were small, thoughtful gifts for everyone, a proof of Grandma Jamila's enduring love: a handmade floral quilt for Ramlah; for Umar, a vintage compass paired with a crafted pen; a cherished recipe book filled with family recipes for Ummi; a leather-bound personal planner for Abbi, reflecting his love for writing; and for Grandpa Luqman, a framed photograph capturing a treasured memory, a reminder of their everlasting love.

Everyone stood still as Abdullah carefully unsealed the first envelope. *"Dear Abdullah, my brave lion,"* the letter began. His grandmother's familiar words echoed within, as though she was still with him. She spoke of his kindness, curious nature, and warm heart that touched everyone he met. The letter extended to each member of the family, highlighting their unique traits, strong love, and most importantly their unity in faith. But it was her closing words that left a permanent mark on his heart.

"My dear Abdullah, promise me this: Be curious, ask questions, embrace love, and leave a legacy while you still can. Time is but a fleeting gift, and our purpose is to worship Allah alone with excellence, sincerity, and wisdom, while accepting His Qadr. Be proud of your identity, wherever you are. Abdullah, my dear. I know your love for bees and honey since you were little. I gathered 100 jars just for you, for I believe you'll carry on my legacy someday. You'll know what to do. Remember, good things happen when the energy of the youth cooperate with the wisdom of the elders."

Tears formed in Abdullah's eyes, and he was not alone in his emotions. "MOWOOWW!" Miza's meow startled everyone, breaking the seriousness with laughter. Then unexpectedly, Yusuf showed up with his little sister, "Are we late for the camping trip?" he grinned.

"Camping's on?!" Abdullah looked at Abbi, surprised.

Abbi playfully replied, "Last to get their camping kit is king of the barn!" They all raced inside, fits of laughter. The legacy of Grandma Jamila lived on, in the letters she left behind and the faith and love that brought her family closer together. Beneath the lunar light, the Hakeem's journey was just beginning, with many stories yet to unfold, and many legacies to build.

GLOSSARY:

Tawheed: Allah is the only Lord of creation. He alone is the Provider and Sustainer. Allah has Names and Attributes that none of the creation share and Allah is to be singled out for worship, alone. Tawheed is maintaining the Oneness of Allah in all the categories mentioned above. Islam makes a clear distinction between the Creator and the created
Allah: The Name of The One True God
Insha'Allah: If Allah Wills
Subhan Allah: Glory be to Allah
Abbi: My father
Ummi: My mother
Wudhu: Ritual ablution
Yallah: Come on
Habibi: My love
Maqluba: An Arabic dish
Kanafeh: An Arabic dessert
Baqlava: A Turkish dessert
Dua: Supplication
Isha: Name of the fifth obligatory prayer of the day
Witr: Name of the odd night prayer
Fajr: Name of the first obligatory prayer of the day
Shakshouka: An Arabic dish
Janazah: Funeral
Ajwa: A type of date
Qiblah: The direction one faces during the prayer (towards Makkah)
Imam: A term that is generally used to refer to the one who leads the prayer. The word is also used to refer to leaders in certain circumstances as well as prestigious scholars
Iman: Belief
Sadaqah: Anything given in charity (applies to all good deeds too)
Merhaba: Hello (Turkish)
Assalamu Alaikum: Islamic greeting 'Peace be upon you all'
Wa Alaikum Salam: Islamic greeting 'And Peace be upon you all'
Quran: Speech of Allah, Revelation from Allah
Sunnah/Hadith: Teachings, sayings, approval of the Prophet
Salaf: Predecessors; the early Muslims of the first three generations; the companions, the Successors and their successors
Islam: To worship Allah alone and not join partners with Him
Astaghfirullah: I seek forgiveness from Allah
Ramadan: The ninth month of the Islamic calendar during which the Muslims fast
Hajj: Pilgrimage to Makkah
Alhamdulillah: All Praise is due to Allah
Masjid: Mosque, place of worship for Muslims
Jumuah: Friday
Ghusl: A ritual bath
Siwak: A twig used for oral hygiene
Iqamah: The call to prayer
Khutbah: A religious talk (sermon) i.e., the khutbah of Jumu'ah
Khateeb: The one delivering the sermon
Hijrah: Migration
Qadr: Allah's Pre-decree and pre-estimation of the creation
Ayah: Sign, miracle, example, lesson. A verse of the Quran

REFERENCES: Below is a list of sources used as proof for the information given in this book:

1. Garment length: Hadith: English Translation of Sunan Abu Dawud, Volume 4, The Book of Clothing, Hadith 4084, 4085, 4086, 4087, 4093.
2. Mention of bees: Quran: Surah An-Nahl, Ayah 68-69.
3. Obedience to parents: Quran: Surah Al-Isra, Ayah 23-24.
4. Being good to parents, the poor, neighbours: Quran: Surah An-Nisa, Ayah 36.
5. Obey Allah, His Messenger, and all those in authority: Quran: Surah An-Nisa, Ayah 59.
6. Obligation for men to pray at the Masjid: Hadith: English Translation of Sahih Muslim, Volume 2, Masajid and Places of Prayer, Hadith [1481] 251 - (651).
7. Oneness of Allah: Quran: Surah Al-Ikhlas.
8. Crying is a mercy: Hadith: Sahih Al-Bukhari Translation Arabic-English, Volume 2, The Book of Funeral, Hadith [1303].
9. To Allah we belong, to Allah we return: Quran: Surah Al-Baqarah, Ayah 156.
10. Obligatory prayers: Quran: Surah Al-Baqarah, Ayah 238, Surah Taha, Ayah 130, Surah Al-Hud, Ayah 114.
11. Dua: May Allah magnify your reward: An-Nawawi in Kitaab Al-Adhkaar.
12. Best dinar a man can spend is on his family: Hadith: English Translation of Sunan Ibn Majah, Volume 4, Chapters of Jihad, Hadith 2760.
13. Allah is the best of planners: Quran Surah Al-Anfal, Ayah 30.
14. Muslim identity: Allah chose Islam as your religion: Quran: Surah Al-Maeda, Ayah 3.
15. Morning Dua upon waking up (and going to sleep): Hadith: Sahih Al-Bukhari Translation Arabic-English, Volume 8, The Book of Invocations, Hadith [6012].
16. Recite the Quran: Quran: Surah Al-Alaq, Ayah 1-5, Surah Al-Muzzammil, Ayah 4.
17. Ajwa dates protect from harm: Hadith: Sahih Al-Bukhari Translation Arabic-English, Volume 7, The Book of Medicine, Hadith [5768].
18. Allah does not punish for shedding tears: Hadith: Sahih Al-Bukhari Translation Arabic-English, Volume 2, The Book of Funeral, Hadith [1304].
19. With every hardship, there is ease: Quran: Surah Al-Inshirah.
20. When a man dies all his good deeds come to an end except three: Sunan An-Anasa'i compiled by Imam Hafiz Abu Abdur Rahman Ahmad bin Shu"aib bin 'Ali An-Nasa'i, Translated by Nasiruddin al-Khattab [Volume 4, The Book of Wills, Chapter 8, The Virtue of Charity Given on Behalf of The Deceased, Hadith 3681, Page 371].
21. Janazah prayer: Hadith: English Translation of Jami' At-Tirmidhi, Volume 2, Chapters of Janaiz, Hadith 1027.
22. Right of every Muslim: Hadith: Sahih Al-Bukhari Translation Arabic-English, Volume 2, The Book of Funeral, Hadith [1239, 1240].
23. Honey has healing properties: Quran: Surah An-Nahl, Ayah 69.
24. Segregation among non-mahram men & women: Quran: Surah Al-Ahzab, Ayah 53.
25. When night falls, keep your children close to you: Hadith: Sahih Al-Bukhari Translation Arabic-English, Volume 4, The Book of The Beginning of Creation, Hadith [3280].
26. Repenting to Allah from sins: Quran: Surah At-Tahrim, Ayah 8.
27. O Allah, forgive our living and our dead: Hadith: English Translation of Jami' At-Tirmidhi, Volume 2, Chapters of Janaiz, Hadith 1024.
28. May peace be upon you, O people of this abode: Hadith: English Translation of Sunan Ibn Majah, Volume 2, Chapters Regarding Funerals, Hadith 1574.
29. O Allah forgive them, O Allah have mercy on them: Hadith: English Translation of Sahih Muslim, Volume 2, The Book of Funerals, Hadith [2232] 85 - (963).
30. Frist foundation of Islam (know Allah): Quran: Surah Fatiha, Ayah 1, Surah Ikhlas.
31. Second foundation of Islam (know the Prophet): Quran: Surah At-Tawba, Ayah 128.
32. Third foundation of Islam (know our religion): Quran: Surah Adh-Dhariyat, Ayah 56.
33. Five Pillars of Islam: Hadith: Sahih Al-Bukhari Translation Arabic-English, Volume 1, The Book of Belief (i.e. Faith), Hadith [8].
34. True belief and action upon that: Quran: Surah Al-Asr.
35. Investigate the truth: Quran: Surah Al-Hujurat, Ayah 6.
36. Letting go of piling up of worldly things: Quran: Surah At-Takathur.
37. The Prophets do not leave behind Dinar or Dirham. The legacy of the scholars is knowledge: Hadith: English Translation of Jami' At-Tirmidhi, Volume 5, Chapters on Knowledge, Hadith 2682 *(Da'if)*.
38. Scholars are the inheritors of the prophets: Quran: Surah Fatir, Ayah 32.
39. Sadaqah applies to all good deeds: Hadith: English Translation of Sahih Muslim, Volume 3, The Book of Zakat, Hadith [2335] 56 - (1009).
40. Beware of suspicion: Hadith: Sahih Al-Bukhari Translation Arabic-English, Volume 8, The Book of Good Manners, Hadith [6066].

41. Importance of being honest, truthful: Hadith: English Translation of Sahih Muslim, Volume 6, The Book of Al-Birr, Hadith [6637] 103 - (2607).
42. Holding on to religion is like holding onto hot coal: Hadith: English Translation of Jami' At-Tirmidhi, Volume 5, Chapters of The Tafsir of Quran, Hadith 3058.
43. Lying is not lawful except in three: Hadith: English Translation of Jami' At-Tirmidhi, Volume 4, Chapters of Righteousness, Hadith 1939.
44. Support like Khadijah (may Allah be pleased with her): Hadith: Sahih Al-Bukhari Translation Arabic-English, Volume 6, The Book of Commentary, Hadith [4953].
45. Putting your trust in Allah: Quran: Surah Al-Ahzab, Ayah 3.
46. Mourning period: Hadith: Sahih Al-Bukhari Translation Arabic-English, Volume 7, The Book of Divorce, Hadith [5339, 5340].
47. Visiting the graves: Hadith: English Translation of Sunan Abu Dawud, Volume 3, The Book of Funerals, Hadith 3235.
48. Reminder about death in Surah Nahl: Quran: Surah Nahl, Ayah 70.
49. Saying 'Jazak Allahu Khair' (May Allah reward you with good): Sunan An-Anasa'i compiled by Imam Hafiz Abu Abdur Rahman Ahmad bin Shu''aib bin 'Ali An-Nasa'i, Translated by Nasiruddin al-Khattab [Volume 1, The Book of Purification, Chapter 204, One Who Cannot Find Water or Clean Earth, Hadith 324, Page 202].
50. Allah grants wisdom to whom He pleases: Quran: Surah Al-Baqarah, Ayah 269.
51. Friday prayer obligation: Quran: Surah Jumuah, Ayah 9-10.
52. Etiquettes of Friday prayer: Hadith: Sahih Al-Bukhari Translation Arabic-English, Volume 2, The Book of Al-Jumuah, Hadith [880].
53. Reward for Friday etiquettes: Hadith: English Translation of Sunan Ibn Majah, Volume 2, Chapters of Establishing…, Hadith 1097.
54. Dua for entering and exiting the Masjid: Hadith: English Translation of Sunan Abu Dawud, Volume 2, The Book of Salat, Hadith 465.
55. Call upon Allah and He will respond: Quran: Surah Ghafir, Ayah
56. Showing mercy to the young and respect to the elders: Hadith: English Translation of Sunan Abu Dawud, Volume 5, The Book of Etiquette, Hadith 4943.
57. Pronounce the Adhan and Iqamah, and the oldest leads the prayer: Hadith: Sahih Al-Bukhari Translation Arabic-English, Volume 1, The Book of Adhan, Hadith [630].
58. Best rows for men are the front rows: Hadith: English Translation of Sunan Ibn Majah, Volume 2, Chapters of Establishing…, Hadith 1000.
59. Every soul shall taste death: Quran: Surah Aalee-Imran, Ayah 185.
60. Allah takes away knowledge by taking the scholars: Hadith: English Translation of Jami' At-Tirmidhi, Volume 5, Chapters on Knowledge, Hadith 2652.
61. Obligation of Hijrah: Hadith: English Translation of Sunan Abu Dawud, Volume 3, The Book of Jihad, Hadith 2479.
62. Be careful with your trust, judge fairly: Quran: Surah An-Nisa, Ayah 58-59.
63. Say 'Our Lord is Allah', and stand firm: Quran: Surah Al-Ahqaf, Ayah 13.
64. The Prophet used not to reject the gifts of perfume: Hadith: Sahih Al-Bukhari Translation Arabic-English, Volume 3, The Book of Gifts, Hadith [2582].
65. We are like travellers (strangers): Hadith: Sahih Al-Bukhari Translation Arabic-English, Volume 8, The Book of Softening of The Hearts, Hadith [6416].
66. Tests prepare us for rewards: Quran: Surah Al-Baqarah, Ayah 155-157.
67. Musa's Dua 'O Allah open for me my chest…': Quran: Surah Taha, Ayah 25-28.
68. All of the believer's affairs are good: Hadith: English Translation of Sahih Muslim, Volume 7, The Book of Asceticism, Hadith [7500] 64 - (2999).
69. Standing firm for justice: Quran: Surah An-Nisa, Ayah 135.
70. Correcting people publicly for the safety of others: Quran: Surah An-Nisa, Ayah 83.
71. Rain is a Mercy: Hadith: English Translation of Sahih Muslim, Volume 2, The Book of Prayer Seeking Rain, Hadith [2084] 14 - (899), [2085] 15 - (...).
72. Each one of you is a shepherd, and will be questioned…: Hadith: English Translation of Sunan Abu Dawud, Volume 3, The Book of Leadership, Hadith 2928.
73. Importance of keeping promises: Quran: Surah Al-Isra, Ayah 34.
74. Disliking a thing that is good for you: Quran: Surah Al-Baqarah, Ayah 216.
75. Inheritance: Quran: Surah An-Nisa, Ayah 11.
76. Allah created you to worship Him alone: Quran: Surah Adh-Dhariyat, Ayah 56.

Note: Please refer to authentic sources such as: Al-Quran, Sahih Al-Bukhari, Sahih Muslim, Sunan Abu Dawud, Sunan At-Tirmidhi, Sunan An-Nasa'i, Sunan ibn Majah, Musnad Ahmad. Also see: abukhadeejah.com/the-islamic-funeral-simple-step-by-step-guide-download-leaflet/ salaficentre.com/2019/09/21/important-guidance-for-the-youth-of-the-ummah-by-shaikh-saaleh-al-fawzaan-hafidhahullaah/

ABOUT THE AUTHOR:

Umm Assad is an inspired author and nurturing educator, weaving stories and lessons from her rich experiences with the elderly, pre-schoolers, and tweens. Her passion for storytelling and education shines through her diverse works, including engaging children's books, educational resources, and heartfelt poetry. Each piece crafted by Umm Assad is a journey into a world where curiosity sparks learning and imagination takes flight, inviting readers of all ages to explore, grow, and believe. Her dedication to touching young hearts and minds makes her a work beloved in the world of children's literature.

Some of Umm Assad's best-selling titles are the 'Allah is One' Series and 'The Prophet Muhammad.'

Other books by Umm Assad:

You can contact Umm Assad where you can also download your free 'Islamic Activity Pack' to use alongside her books:

Websites:
ummassadpublications.com,
ummassadhomeschool.com

Twitter: ummassadpubs
Instagram: ummassad.pubs
Facebook: ummassadpubs
Youtube: ummassadpublications

ummassadpublications.com
'Take Pride in Authenticity'

Printed in Great Britain
by Amazon